My Goodness

Also by Joe Queenan

Imperial Caddy

If You're Talking to Me, Your Career Must Be in Trouble

The Unkindest Cut

Red Lobster, White Trash, and The Blue Lagoon

Confessions of a Cineplex Heckler

JOE QUEENAN

My Goodness

A Cynic's

Short-lived

Search for

Sainthood

HYPERION
new york

LIBRARY OF CONGRESS CATALOGING-IN-PUBLICATION DATA
Queenan, Joe.
  My goodness: a cynic's short-lived search for sainthood/
by Joe Queenan.
      p.   cm.
1. Queenan, Joe. 2. Journalists—United States—Biography.
3. Journalism—Moral and ethical aspects. 4. Conduct of
life. 5. Social ethics. 6. Misanthrophy. 7. Cynicism. I. Title.
PN4874.Q39 A3 2000
070'.92—dc21
[B]
                                        99-039284
                                           CIP

ISBN 0-7868-6553-9

Book design by Richard Oriolo

First Edition

10 9 8 7 6 5 4 3 2 1

For Gregory, a kindred spirit

The author wishes to thank
Jennifer Barth and Joe Vallely.

Contents

"You're a better man
than I am, Gunga Din."

—Rudyard Kipling

My Goodness

1. Oral History

Since I started out as a writer many years ago, I have built a reputation as an acerbic, mean-spirited observer of the human condition. Although the particular *arc* of my career has brought me a certain celebrity and a measure of wealth, it has not made me a happy person. True, some of my peers generously regard me as a curmudgeon, a gadfly, a well-meaning mad hatter, but in my heart of hearts I know otherwise. My chronic nastiness and obdurate refusal to look on the bright side of things goes far beyond garden-variety misanthropy. In a very real sense, I am a complete and utter bastard.

One reason I became a full-time son of a bitch and have never deviated from my chosen career as a sneering churl is because the money is so good. In a world where most journalists are more than happy to service movie stars, captains of industry, and people like Bill Moyers, I have carved out a financially remunerative niche as one of the handful of hired guns that editors can turn to when they need a fast, efficient hatchet job. The truth is, there simply aren't that many American journalists who are as consistently and methodically unaccommodating as me. Most writers would get tired of being so uniformly and predictably contemptuous of everything and everybody. Most people wouldn't be able to sleep at night. But I have always been able to sleep at night. In fact, I have always slept rather well.

In late 1998, however, I began to succumb to the cumulative effects of a lifetime spent being clinically unpleasant. As I approached my fiftieth year and felt the footsteps of mortality just a few yards in my wake, I found myself questioning whether I wanted to spend the rest of my life as a human adder. When I read about Jimmy Carter's gallant efforts to rebuild defective roofs in the South Bronx, or Sting's courageous attempts to save the rain forest, or Susan Sarandon's selfless efforts on behalf of Death Row denizens, the homeless, the infirm, the…(well, you get the idea), there was a part of me that was deeply envious of their activities. It wasn't so much that I actually *wanted to* repair roofs in the South Bronx or give aid and comfort to contrite, albeit convicted, rapists and murderers or help to save the rain forest; it's just that I thought people would like and respect me a whole lot more if I wasn't such a complete deadbeat. I was tired of people telling me that I was clever; I wanted people to start telling me that I was good.

Was there a specific event that precipitated my Saul of Tarsus-like conversion to the path of righteousness? Yes, there was. One night, in the fall of 1998, I purchased a ridiculously expensive tube of Tom's of Maine toothpaste. In doing so, I was out on a search-and-destroy mission. A couple of years earlier, my wife and I had been roped into attending a speech by Tom Chappell, founder and CEO of the world's most socially conscious toothpaste company. For forty-five minutes, I had sat in my chair yawning and grimacing as Tom of Maine yammered on and on about his "mission," his "vocation," his "journey," his wife Kate's poetry, and his company's principled refusal to experiment on lab animals, as if anyone in the room cared one way or the other about the plight of a few disgusting rats. Remarking to my wife, "Where's Lee Harvey Oswald when you really need him?" I made a mental note to double back when I had some spare time and give Tom of Maine, Kate of Maine, and Anybody Else of Maine Who Thought They Were Better than Me Just Because They Didn't Experiment on Lab Animals a good journalistic thrashing. And now, two years later, that time had come.

On first glance, the toothpaste container seemed to provide me with plenty of material for target practice. Neatly tucked inside was a little note to consumers explaining, in typical blowhard fashion, the special social "mission" of the company. Then there was extensive information about the National Anti-Vivisection Society and the American Anti-Vivisection Society, including 800 numbers and website addresses where ordinary people could learn more about the systematic abuse of lab animals by Tom's of Maine's competitors. Finally, there was a grammatically disastrous hand-written note from a little girl named Kim telling Tom and Kate just how wonderful they were. As if they needed to be told.

Loaded up with this ammo, I trained my sights on these infuriatingly self-congratulatory targets, who, much like Ben & Jerry and Anita Roddick and Susan Sarandon and Sting, seemed completely incapable of scooping up a piece of litter or giving a blind dwarf a nickel without issuing a twelve-page press release apprising the general public of their awesome munificence. A Roman Catholic in spirit, if not in practice, that rankled. My thoughts drifted back to character-molding Biblical passages I had learned in my youth:

God, I thank thee that I am not as other men are: extortioners, unjust, adulterers, or even as the publican. I fast twice in the week, I give tithes of all that I possess.

And:

Therefore, when thou doest thine alms, do not sound a trumpet before thee, as the hypocrites do in the synagogue and in the streets.

And:

For everyone that exalteth himself shall be abased, and he that humbleth himself shall be exalted.

Since I seemed to have both God the Father and God the Son in my corner as I planned my imminent evisceration of these self-aggrandizing do-gooders, I couldn't wait to get to my PC the next day. But then I had a change of heart. What, after all, was so wrong with using one's celebrity and even one's merchandise to better the human condition and make this a better planet? Sure, the Good Book said that charity vaunteth not itself. But that was back in olden days when charity-vaunting was anathema in the eyes of Yahweh. Things were different today. Back in Biblical times, mankind was not trying to destroy the rain forest or melt the polar ice cap or torment twenty million lab animals every year just to make cheaper toothpaste or snazzier perfume. Back in Biblical times, famous people could afford to keep their good works under their hat or their bushel, because the fate of the earth was not yet in the balance. But times had changed, and the Toms of Maine were the first to recognize that. Typically, I was among the last.

But there was more to it than that; I had selfish reasons for changing my tune. When I conjured up a mental image of Tom of Maine rhapsodizing about his cruelty-free products or Ben & Jerry marketing a flavor that promoted world peace or Sting doing a benefit concert to help save the rain forest, what I saw were happy, vibrant, upbeat people. When I looked at my own personality, what I saw was a shriveled-up old prune. And I was dog-tired of being a shriveled-up old prune.

And so, I decided to set out on the road to spiritual self-regeneration, to transform myself into the very best human being I could be. On the most obvious level, this would involve being more generous to the people I wrote about. I would have to start writing *positive* book reviews in the *New York Times* and the *Wall Street Journal* and publishing *enthusiastic* interviews with celebrities. I would have to say *life-affirming* things about the businessmen I wrote about in *Barron's* and *Forbes*, and stop tearing things down simply for the sake of a few cheap laughs. After all these years of spewing venom, Old Mister Grumpy Face was getting shown to the door.

Of course, there would be more, much more. There would be

volunteer work at civic organizations, immense activity on behalf of the snail darter, the manatees, the Dalai Lama, and any other Lamas who crossed my path. In the fullness of time, once my incipient goodness had become second-nature to me, I might even establish my own foundation to benefit the needy, the infirm, or the just plain dumb. (*Oops, there I go again!*) I would carefully study the exploits of positive role models like Peter Gabriel, Jimmy Carter, and Alec Baldwin, and attempt to emulate their radiant *bonhomie*. Ultimately, I might even seek instruction from religious leaders on how I could prepare myself for early sainthood.

From the very start, I decided that in attempting to transform myself into a spectacular human being, I would be careful to behave in an *ostentatiously* virtuous fashion. The one thing I had learned over the years from observing the Susan Sarandons and Ben & Jerrys of the world was that there was no point in being a wonderful person unless everyone else knew about it. Believe you me, when I set out on the Road to Perfection, people were going to get all the facts and figures.

In committing myself to this undertaking, I was aware that things might turn out disastrously, that the attempt to turn myself into a unilaterally swell human being could wreck my nervous system and ruin my career. I was prepared to take that risk. I was prepared to do so because I was tired of feeling worthless, because I was tired of being the sourpuss at the wedding feast, and because I did not want to meet my Maker with so few positive accomplishments on my side of the ledger.

Only time would tell whether it was possible for a person as jaded, cynical, and basically horrible as me to effect the transition into transplendent munificence. Frankly, I wasn't going to bet the house on it. But I was willing to give it a try. I have never, ever backed away from a challenge.

Being good was going to be the biggest challenge of my life.

2 · *La Vita è Bruta:*

A Chronicle of

Personal Vileness

The first issue I had to address once I had launched my foray into the subculture of virtue was the central moral paradox in my entire existence—namely: The only reason I was able to take time off to devote myself to the reconstruction of my unacceptable personality was because I was pretty well fixed financially. But the reason I was so well fixed was because I had made tons of money being cruel to people over the years. What's more, many of the people I had gone out of my way to be cruel to were people that I was now starting to revere.

For example, in the previous ten years, I had written five separate stories making fun of Ben & Jerry, and had used them as punching bags or gags in innumerable others. For these stories, I had been paid $12,950. I had also written a number of articles ridiculing Jimmy Carter, for which I had been reimbursed to the tune of $7,000. The abuse of Sting ($4,500), Bono ($4,000), Susan Sarandon ($5,500), and various other indisputably good people had also helped glut my coffers to over-flowing. All told, my scornful treatment of unquestionably good human beings or the causes they supported had earned me $68,687, enough to buy two Toyota Previa vans.

I had, in fact, bought one Previa van, fully equipped, and had put the rest into blue-chip stocks trading at reasonably low multiples, plus a few small-cap cyclicals. And therein lay the supreme irony: that I was now buying Ben & Jerry's ice cream and Sting CDs with the very same money I had made by mocking them. That is, the money plus the vast appreciation in the value of my portfolio, bloated with stocks I had been wise enough to buy with the Dow at 3700, even though they included ethically fetid corporations which derived their earnings from the sale of tobacco, alcohol, and armaments. True, nobody ever said life was fair. But this seemed hideously unfair.

On the subject of revenue flows, it should be noted that not all of my income had been derived from eviscerating superb human beings such as Ben & Jerry and Susan Sarandon. Over the years, I had written many acerbic stories about crooked stock promoters, New Age charla-tans, cretinous movie stars, dim-witted politicians, uncharismatic canni-bals, and John Tesh. I felt no remorse whatsoever over these stories. I did not feel bad about the $3,000 I'd earned from the *Movieline* story "Mickey Rourke for a Day," nor about the $15,000 I had earned from the British TV program it was repackaged into. I did not regret the tens of thousands of dollars I'd made pillorying Chuck Norris, Tori Spelling, Andrew Lloyd Webber, and Deepak Chopra. And I certainly felt no remorse about the $43,000 I had made fish-gutting Geraldo.

And yet…and yet. In my heart of hearts, I knew that much of what I was doing here was rationalizing. Sure, I had devoted a lot of my time and energy to eviscerating the Michaels Bolton, Jackson, and Milken, not to mention the Kennys Rogers, Loggins, and G. But how much of my rancor had been directed at cultural vermin such as these, and how much had been consumed by capricious attacks on undeserving victims? For that matter, what percentage of my stories had been mean-spirited? How many had been demonstrably unfair? Precisely how awful a man was this Joe Queenan?

It was a quandary that would become an obsession over the next few weeks. The big problem was that I didn't have any hard data, and procuring it was not going to be easy. I had started my career as a journalist in June 1986, when I published an acrid but thought-provoking op-ed piece in the *Wall Street Journal* entitled "Ten Things I Hate About Public Relations." Over the next twelve years I had written 889 stories for such top-flight publications as *GQ*, the *New York Times*, *Spy*, *Barron's*, the *Washington Post*, and *Forbes*, as well as for less well-known publications such as *Chief Executive*, *Commonweal*, *Venture*, and *Amtrak Express*. I had also written three original books. That worked out to 5,438 type-written pages of magazine and newspaper articles plus another 969 pages of book manuscript pages, for a grand total of 6,407 pages. I had also written one full-length screenplay and three half-hour screenplays, but because very few people saw my movie and the three short films aired only in Great Britain, I decided to set them to the side.

Estimating that a single typewritten page averages 225 words, this meant that in the previous twelve years I had written 1,441,575 words, and it was a safe bet that just about all of them had been unpleasant. Or let's just say that most of them had been used in the construction of a nasty sentence, phrase, paragraph, or chapter. Since I am not a good typist, hunting and pecking out perhaps thirty words a minute, this meant that I had spent 48,095 minutes—or 801 hours, or twenty complete working weeks—doing nothing but being vicious. And that didn't include time for research, fact-checking, travel, and lunch. Plus going to Los Angeles to be vicious on *Politically Incorrect*.

For a number of reasons, I was determined to find out how many of these words had actually been cruel. Well, maybe not how many words in and of themselves had been cruel ("the" and "an" lack the inherent venom of "moron" and "schmuck"), but how many words had been used in the construction of sentences deliberately fabricated with malicious intent.

Compiling this data was not going to be easy. To do so, I would have to review every sentence in every story I had ever written and tabulate my offenses. This would take weeks, perhaps months. Frankly, I had no appetite for this project, because rereading everything I had ever written just to see how cruel I had been would be psychologically debilitating, like an ax murderer visiting the tombs of his victims. Moreover, all the time I would spend calculating how beastly I had been in the past was time that could be put to better use doing good deeds in the present.

To avoid all this paperwork, I set myself the task of devising rigorous mathematical formulas to determine how many contemptible things I had said, how frequently I had said them, and the relative virulence of each statement I had made. Here again I hit a roadblock. On first thought, it seemed logical that if I took a random sample of my stories and counted how many hostile things I had said on each page, then multiplied it by a suitable coefficient, I would arrive at a figure quantifying both the number of nasty remarks and the ratio of mean things to inoffensive or nice things I had said over the years.

Unfortunately, not all of my stories were equally unpleasant. The articles I had written for *Movieline*, *Spy*, the *Wall Street Journal*, and *GQ* tended to be fiendishly nasty, while the work I had done for *TV Guide*, the *New York Times*, and the *Washington Post* was, in general, more nuanced, delicate, reasoned, balanced. In the latter, I tended to use a battle-ax; in the former, a hydrogen bomb. Thus, in order for my survey to purport to any methodological validity whatsoever, I had to make sure that the work was assayed in the correct proportion. Since one-sixth of my work had appeared in *Movieline*, one sixth in *Barron's*, and one sixth in my three books, it was imperative that half the material under examination come from these sources.

There was another problem. Even though I was sincere in my intention to become a better person, there nevertheless lay a sediment of putrescent bile at the core of my very personality. My idea of what was ill-natured would be very different from the average person's. If I went through my stories highlighting all the cruel things I had ever written, I would end up with a much smaller number than the ordinary layman. But which figure would be the correct one?

To address this problem, I decided to send out a representative selection of my work to a statistically relevant group of my friends (30) and have them analyze how inhumane I had been. This required elbow grease. I spent the better part of an entire weekend divvying up my work into three basic groups—Mean, Very Mean, and Unconscionable —then divided up my friends into similar categories: Nice, Okay, and Horrible. Once the selection process was complete, I sent each of these thirty friends roughly 5,000 words (20 pages) of my output. This came to 150,000 words or 600 pages, roughly 10 percent of my *oeuvre*. It was my intention to study their cumulative responses, tally up the incidents of malice, divide the total number of mean remarks by the total number of sentences in each story, and then multiply that by ten to determine

1) How many nasty things I had said in my career.

2) How frequently I had said nasty things.

3) The ratio of sentences containing nasty remarks to those containing generally inoffensive material.

The manila envelopes that I sent out were accompanied by this letter:

> Dear Friend:
>
> As part of a massive project I am currently working on, I need to quantify exactly how many genuinely unpleasant things I have said in my career. Accordingly, I am distributing my work to a wide array of friends, seeking their feedback. Could you please take the time to read the enclosed material and underline or highlight every remark that could reasonably be interpreted as being mean-spirited, in the sense that it was definitely meant to inflict harm? I stress that the intent of the writer, rather than the appropriateness of the target, is the main issue here; even if the remark was directed at someone as odious as Benito Mussolini, Attila the Hun, or Geraldo Rivera, I would still like you to make a note of it. Also, any comments would be helpful.

I thank you in advance for your help in this massive undertaking.

Best Wishes,

Joe Queenan

Now I had to wait. And wait. And wait some more. Yes, although some of my friends sent the material back like a shot, recognizing that this was a serious request, many more of them dawdled for weeks on end, and some did not even bother to reply. By failing to do so, these craven individuals catastrophically undermined the methodological validity of my study, thus imperiling our friendship. But in the end this did not matter because the people who did reply weren't much more helpful. Some people underlined almost everything. Some people underlined almost nothing. Some people took offense at the use of the term "forked tongue," while others let "cocksucker" slip right by. One of my friends said she was too busy to review the material, so she got her assistant to do it. Needless to say, she works in the entertainment industry.

The biggest failing of my informal survey, one that I had anticipated and perhaps even feared, was that my assorted friends had very different levels of sensitivity to cruelty. Take, for example, my ex-dear friend Andy Ferguson, who works for Rupert Murdoch's satanic *Weekly Standard* and who once wrote speeches for George Bush.

Andy, a persnickety sort, had technical problems with my request. Though he found that "mean-spiritedness permeated the pieces like a fog, like some kind of untraceable mephitic stench," he was disappointed that he could not find "specific insults directed at specific individuals whom you clearly intended to make feel bad." And he still wonders why Bush lost.

Another friend wrote that since everything I said was deliberately spiteful, she didn't feel like wasting her time highlighting every single sentence. A third friend said that she could not in conscience highlight or underscore insults directed at people who clearly deserved to be insulted, even though I had specifically requested that my friends draw attention to every mean remark, no matter whom it was directed at, *because that was the whole point of the exercise.* And a fourth friend said that the entire procedure was pointless because I was a "nasty fuck" and didn't need to conduct a scientific study to figure that out.

Finally, there were the fussbudgets. Some people sent pages and pages of notes and even footnotes. Others suggested ways that my writing could have been even nastier. Oh great: *The Amateur Hour.* Most meticulous of all was Doug Colligan, a friend who works at *Reader's Digest*, but who is probably best remembered for his eccentric, catatonic interpretation of Dr. Paul Thorpe in my doomed $7,000 movie *Twelve Steps to Death.* Doug couldn't resist getting out the colored pens: blue for generally inoffensive remarks, red for when folks got smacked around a little, orange for when things really started to get personal, Day-Glo Yellow for when people got completely hammered, orange-and-yellow for pure viciousness, and blue-red-yellow for nuclear *ad hominem* slander. Like I needed this hassle.

In the end, as usual, my friends proved completely worthless. Once again, I learned the hard way that if you wanted something done right, you had to do it yourself. So now I finally did what I had been moving heaven and earth to avoid: I made a pile of everything I had ever written, got out a load of colored pens, turned on the calculator, turned off the phones, and got hard to work.

The results were not as bad as I had expected. Start with film criticism. Between 1994 and 1998, I had written forty-two movie reviews, totaling 170 pages, for the British paper the *Guardian.* Of these reviews, seventeen had been positive, twenty had been negative, and five were mixed. The positive reviews included *The Bridges of Madison County* and *Dumb and Dumber,* which critics like me were supposed to hate, while the negative reviews included *Mighty Aphrodite, The Ice Storm, Good Will Hunting,* and *Jefferson in Paris,* which critics like me were supposed to love. Since 70 percent of commercially produced movies are atrocious, twenty bad reviews out of forty-two was by no means a high number. In fact, it was a low number.

Obviously, my positive reviews contained much material that was negative, since I often waged literary proxy wars, using praise of an actor or director I admired to flail away at an actor or director I despised. Because of this, a nine-hundred-word "positive" review might still contain ten to twenty nasty remarks. This did not change the fact that the reviews were themselves positive.

I was similarly heartened by my book reviews. Between 1986 and 1998, I had written 217 book reviews, of which 79 were generally positive, while 138 were mostly negative. This meant that *in toto* 572 pages, or approximately 8 percent, of my life's work had been devoted to slamming books. In my defense, many of these books were pure slag that anyone would have pummeled, written as they were by unsuccessful human beings such as Ivan Boesky or the road manager for Led Zeppelin. True, I had gone out of my way to be beastly to Stephen King, Robert Ludlum, Newt, and Geraldo, but I certainly wasn't going to lose any sleep over that. What I was losing sleep over was my massacre of books by morally impeccable people such as Ben & Jerry, Mia Farrow, Anita Roddick, Kitty Dukakis, and Jimmy Carter. For this I felt most abjectly penitent.

Setting aside my despair, I proceeded to a more general analysis of my work. Organized purely by genre, there were 105 stories, comprising 558 pages, that could honestly be described as Good Clean Fun or Innocuous Frou-Frou, where I did not go out of my way to be mean to anyone in particular. These stories included a *Washington Post* article about the Cosa Nostra's introduction of a casual Fridays dress code, a *New Republic* story about how Japanese satirists with names like Yukio "The Human Whoopie Cushion" Hirodaki were taking over the U.S. satire business by dumping their jokes on the market, and "I Married an Accountant," a *Newsweek* account of fascinating accountants I had known and, in one case, married. This was standard, rib-tickling fare, where the satire focused on amusing human foibles, the language was suffused with a lighthearted bonhomie, and no attempt was made to inflict pain.

Next there were fifty-three articles, comprising some 480 pages, in which I had simply Taken the Mickey out of People. These stories, ranging from a *GQ* account of being a slacker for a week to a story about my desire for a National Bond Market Appreciation Day, were good-natured little numbers where I may have ruffled a few feathers and taken individuals or institutions down a peg or two but generally tried to keep the negativity to a minimum. For instance, one story poked fun at culture vultures by falsely reporting that an art phone in a Boston Museum was telling museum goers that the men in all those Winslow Homer fishing boats were actually gay landlubbers meeting for assignations off the coast of sexually repressed 19th-century Boston, where homosexuality was still illegal. Harmless stuff, good for a few chuckles, but ever so slightly *edgier* than the Good, Clean Fun category.

I had also written seventeen pieces, mostly for *Barron's,* that were basically Straight Reporting about IBM, the prosecution of Mike Milken, or explanations of concepts such as leveraged buyouts. In these stories, which ran to 204 pages, the chuckles were kept to an absolute minimum. However, because the total volume of this uncharacteristically straightforward material was only 3.3 percent of my life's work, I did not feel that it skewed the study in any great way, being more than offset by the statistical overload of plain, old-fashioned cussedness in my *Movieline, Spy,* and *GQ* pieces.

Seventeen stories totaling 210 pages fell into the Service Piece category. These included a fawning *GQ* travel piece about Jamaica, a fawning *GQ* story about learning to golf, and a fawning *GQ* story about an almost mythical New York salon that had just started marketing its services to men. Ironically, the day after the story ran I received a handwritten note from the proprietor of the salon telling me how much he liked the story. Ironically, the day after that, the salon burned to the ground.

The next category is best described as Profiles that Couldn't Help but Make the Subject Happy. Over the years, I had written twelve of these stories, totaling 134 pages, covering everyone from the founder of the first astrologically oriented mutual fund to the man who invented the *Time* magazine cover-story indicator (if *Time* says the bull market is over, buy stocks), to an options trader who left AMEX forever to study theology after getting blown out in DEC puts. These stories contained heaping portions of humor, but were rarely malicious, and nothing untoward was ever said about the person who was the subject of the profile.

In a slightly different category were Quirky Stories that Told You

Something You Might Not Otherwise Have Known. These included a *Forbes* article about why buying Lionel Ritchie's autograph was such a poor investing decision and a couple of whimsical op-ed pieces of the Oh, Those Brits! variety. There were fourteen of these, and all told they came to eighty-eight pages.

A much larger category, consisting of 158 stories and running to 680 pages, was Pedagogical Satire. This group consisted of informative and/or amusing stories in which the overall tone was sneering, but the contempt was used to inform, admonish, cajole, correct a misimpression, take the wind out of bloated sails, redress the balance, or make a larger point. Typical items included a *Philadelphia* magazine article providing scientific proof that downtown Philly was still as boring as it was when I was growing up there despite the City That Loves You Back's energetic attempts to persuade people otherwise, a *TV Guide* story about being Martha Stewart for a day, and a *Spy* exposé about calling up a bunch of brokerage houses and asking if they would help me to go public with a chain of medieval amusement parks called Plague World. The object here was to edify by amusing, and in each case the targets of my criticism had brought any possible embarrassment upon themselves by being duplicitous, dumb, or Martha Stewart.

Another category consisted of Undeniably Mean Stories Where I Nevertheless Occupied the Moral High Ground. There were sixty of them, comprising 569 pages, and they included:

- An indictment of PBS for using taxpayers' hard-earned money to advance John Tesh's career.

- Innumerable attacks on Hollywood for allowing mindless violence to masquerade as art.

- An indictment of white rock critics who go out of their way to fellate rappers.

- Various stories about crooked stock promoters, sleazy entrepreneurs, intrepid scamsters, outright dicks.

- Assorted stories about unethical journalists, dishonest politicians, garden-variety scoundrels.

- Several stories about Fergie.

- Several stories about Mickey Rourke.

The next category (eleven articles, 120 pages) consisted of Entertainment Industry Pieces Where I Thought I Was Being Pretty Nice to the Subjects, but They May Have Felt Otherwise. These included *Movieline* profiles of Jessica Lange, Keanu Reeves, and Spike Lee; a *Rolling Stone* profile of Renny Harlin; and assorted *TV Guide* items praising figures as varied as Mary Steenburgen, Charles Grodin, Larry King, and George Segal. The fact that some of these people did not like what I wrote about them did not concern me; frankly, I thought they were lucky to get off so lightly.

A very tiny category consisted of valentines—indisputably nice pieces about Frank Sinatra and a recently deceased friend. There were two of these stories, they made up just nine pages of my life's work, and the subjects were already dead when I wrote them. Here I must stress that these stories were valentines, not blow jobs. I have never written for *Vanity Fair* or *Premiere*.

Two very small categories included Stories Where I Made Fun of the French (six articles, twenty-five pages), and Theater Reviews (I saw one play by Steve Tesich and decided never to write another theater review). The next major category was made up of Stories Where I Went Out of My Way to Be Mean to People Who Probably Deserved It, Though Some Might Question this Assessment. Basically, this included the meanest things I had ever written for *Movieline, Spy, GQ,* and *Playboy,* plus a few other items from hither and yon. It consisted of forty stories and took up 560 pages. It was the work I was best known for, and while I now regretted some of the cruel things I had said, I would probably still have laughed had somebody else said them. Frankly, it was hard to feel sorry for people like Sylvester Stallone, Mickey Rourke, Melanie Griffith, Don Johnson, etc.; they had reaped what they had sown.

The final major category is best summed up as Stories Where I Went Out of My Way to Be Mean to People Who Didn't Really Deserve It. It consisted of sixty-five pieces, comprising 386 pages, with my victims ranging from Ben & Jerry to Mother Nature to determined environmentalists to Jimmy Carter. Though my tone ranged from whimsical to shrill, the result was always the same: Somebody got raked over the coals. For example, in the *New Republic* I had once sneered at performers who appeared in benefits such as Farm Aid by writing a fake news story about an event called Certified Financial Planners Aid, attended by Bruce Springsteen, John Cougar Mellencamp, U2, Jackson Browne, Pete Seeger, Kris Kristofferson, Bob Dylan, Joan Baez, Willie Nelson, Crosby, Stills & Nash, Harry Belafonte, Johnny Cash, Ethiopia, the Mormon Tabernacle Choir, and many others. In other articles, I had ridiculed the recovery movement, folksingers, socially conscious investors, environmentalists. I called anti-nuke activist Benjamin Spock a "publicity-hogging old gasbag." I linked working-class hero and citizen activist Bruce Springsteen to insider trader Ivan Boesky via their common friendship with John Mulheren, the risk arbitrageur who once threatened to kill Boesky. I used Salman Rushdie's misfortune as the excuse for a snide story. I made fun of Stephen Hawking's *A Brief History of Time* even though he was in a wheelchair and was probably writing as well as he knew how. I said that if Mother Nature was really our friend, where did AIDS, hurricanes, and smallpox come from? I sneered at Kitty Dukakis and her drinking problem, explaining that I could not help doing so because I was a meanaholic and could not control my impulses. And I pilloried Marcia Clark for losing the least winnable case in the history of American jurisprudence, even though I knew she was trying her level best.

Sometimes, it wasn't just a case of cut-and-dried cruelty. I could also be irresponsible. Once I wrote about organizing death squads to get rid of aging folksingers. Another time I recommended that either Peter or Paul of Peter, Paul & Mary—I can no longer remember which —be lynched. In several instances I called down divine retribution on actors who may not have even believed in the same God as me.

Ultimately, I knew that if I was serious about my conversion to the path of righteousness, I would have to make amends for some of the horrible things I had said about these people. But what form these amends would take I could not yet specify.

• • •

In any event, with my magazine and newspaper work out of the way, it was now time to take a gander at my three original books. Here, again, I was pleasantly surprised by how little of what I had said actually warranted contrition. My first book, *Imperial Caddy,* was a good-natured ribbing of the lunkheaded vice president, but the book was unexpectedly free of malice. Indeed, the only thing in *Imperial Caddy* that I had any second thoughts about was the chapter "To the Hoosier Station," where I portrayed the great state of Indiana (home of Michael Jackson, Jim Jones, John Dillinger, Axl Rose, and the man who wrote "On the Banks of the Wabash") as a hotbed of depravity, violence, and insanity. This was clearly an exaggeration, meant to inflict harm. But because I'd been forced to endure nightly crank phone calls from an irate Hoosier for several weeks after the book appeared, until the police finally traced the call, I felt that I had already paid the price for my light-hearted depredations. Other than that, the book was devoid of gratuitous meanness. Moreover, because it was about a Republican, the potential for gratuitous cruelty warranting contrition was very small indeed.

Slightly more problematic was my 1995 book *The Unkindest Cut,* which recounted my doomed efforts to make a $7,000 movie for under $50,000. The film, *Twelve Steps to Death,* concerns a psychiatrist who is found brutally murdered, with suspicion falling on his patients, all of whom are in 12-step programs. To complicate matters, the police officer investigating the case had lost his wife and two children a few years earlier when they were killed in a hit-and-run accident by a schizoid anorexic recovering alcoholic with attention deficit disorder.

Obviously, both the movie and the book were an excuse for me to tee off on drunks, fat people, fat drunks, cokeheads, the recovery movement in general. But, as far I can tell, I did not mention anyone in particular. If it is any consolation whatsoever, I did not write these nasty remarks just to be mean; I really did hate people in recovery at the time that I wrote this, though in retrospect I now realized that this was a very poor attitude. But since just about nobody bought that book and hardly anyone ever saw the movie, the actual number of real live people harmed by *The Unkindest Cut* and *12 Steps to Death* was so small that there was no reason for me to feel bad about it.

For entirely different reasons, I felt no compunction about any-thing I had said in *Red Lobster, White Trash and the Blue Lagoon.* All told, the book insulted 413 movie stars, directors, authors, singers, politi-cians, and purveyors of middlebrow cuisine. However, unlike much of my other work, where I went out of my way to be unkind to people that most intelligent people would have viewed as good-hearted (Ben & Jerry, Jimmy Carter) or harmless (Susan Sarandon, Sting), *Red Lobster* was an attack on the obviously and indisputably wicked (Geraldo, Garth, Tesh). Since the premise of the book was for me to spend a year immersed in a cultural abyss with Stephen King, Robert James Waller, and Phil Collins, the very notion of feeling regret about what I had writ-ten would suggest that these individuals had not merited execration and a heaping daily gob of spittle.

But this was clearly not the case; the fact that I now recognized what a horrible man I had been all my life did not make any of these people less repellent. Yes, I was bad, but they were worse. Or look at it this way: Just because Joseph Stalin is Adolf Hitler's worst enemy does-n't make the cast of *Riverdance* your best friends. The truth was, *Red Lobster* had been the one time in my career when I had devoted all my talents and energies to attacking a pack of cultural rodents who truly deserved it. So there would be no apologizing here, not even to the fam-ilies of people who had died since the book appeared. Chris Farley's movies didn't get any better just because he was dead. Neither did James Michener's novels or John Denver's songs.

This meticulous breakdown provided a general structural overview of my life's work. But it did not answer the question: How many mean things had I said in the course of my career? The answer: 47,678 nasty remarks, or one cruel remark every two sentences. In my body of work, there were 2,537 ad hominem attacks, 1,123 gratuitous asides, 342 cases of pure slander, and 564 examples of unconscionable cruelty. (There were also 137 canards, more than I had expected.) Roughly 42 percent of my work involved shooting fish in a barrel, set-ting up straw men, or beating a dead horse, with another 23 percent devoted to using sitting ducks, stooges, bozos, schlemiels, ding-dongs, and hapless victims for target practice. The ratio of mean remarks to nice ones was a staggering 9.56 to 1.

Here is a more nuanced breakdown of my life's work:

Obviously Satanic People I Made Fun of

Tull, Mike Milken, Tori Spelling, Ivan Boesky, Dan Dierdorf, Joe Theismann, Howard Cosell, Dennis Rodman, Ross Perot, the Serbs, Fergie, Bill Bennett, Bernadette Peters, the stars of *The Real World*, Guns n' Roses, conservatives who try to dress in hip clothing, the pollster for Gingrich's Contract with America, John Tesh, Newt Gingrich, Michael Bolton, Michael Flatley, Kenny G, Patrick Swayze, Adolf Hitler, Carly Simon, Benito Mussolini, Demi Moore, Attila the Hun, Libby Dole, lots of other Republicans, Miss America, Donald Trump, Karl Marx, all lawyers, short sellers, Al D'Amato, Bill Gates, my fellow journalists, ELO.

Unlikely People I Defended

Accordionists, Jeffrey Dahmer, accountants, perverts who pay taxes and are therefore entitled to have a portion of the NEA budget devoted to the support of disgusting art, Howard Stern, Rosie O'Donnell, the bond market, Bob Barker, Jennie Jones, Klaus Kinski, the United States Department of Agriculture, Barry Manilow, Wayne Newton, Burt Reynolds, bond rating agencies, Charles Grodin, Larry King, CPAs, Nancy Reagan, psychics, the American Dental Association, Lawrence Welk, the guys who built Canary Wharf, Cato, Oliver Cromwell, Dan and Marilyn Quayle, Keanu Reeves, Tom Cruise, Michael Douglas, Julia Roberts.

Cities I Repeatedly Ridiculed, Not without Some Justification, But Perhaps with Excessive Glee

Philadelphia, San Francisco, Raleigh-Durham, Baltimore, Austin, Dallas, Edmonton, and Burlington, Vt.

Icons I Pitilessly Traduced

Bill Moyers, Walter Cronkite, John Chancellor, Woody Allen, James Michener, John Elway (when he was still a choke artist), Mikhail Gorbachev, Albert Camus, Phil Spector, Sonny Bono, Hillary Clinton, Philip Glass, Colin Powell, Arthur Schlesinger Jr., Merchant & Ivory.

Unusually Vicious Ad Hominem Attacks

Raisa Gorbachev (bad dresser), Jesse Kornbluth (idiot), assorted *BusinessWeek* writers (creeps/idiots), Pete Petersen (phony), David Crosby (idiot).

Big Fish Shot in Barrel

Robert Ludlum, Led Zeppelin, flacks, Phil Gramm, Michael Jackson, Ice Cube, Rock Critics, Oliver Stone, Al Gore, Peter Mayle, Tom Peters, the Utah Jazz, Shaquille O'Neal, O.J. Simpson, John Cameron, Lee Iacocca.

Small Fish Shot in Barrel

My computer geek neighbors, Mike Dukakis, the New Jersey Nets, MBAs, outplacement specialists, CBA basketball players, the Houston Oilers, fedora makers, market researchers, people who write manuals for computers and fax machines, the man who designed the leaf blower, ethical auditors, authors of books about reengineering, stockbrokers, NEA officials, focus groups, editors of dipshit literary magazines that turned down my stories when I was first getting started in the business.

Nations Repeatedly or Egregiously Calumnied

The Ukraine, Paraguay, Nigeria, Indonesia, France, Belgium.

A man ought to have more to show for his life than this.

3 • A Short History

of Goodness, from

Jesus Christ to Sting

A famous man whose name presently escapes me once said that he who cannot remember the past is condemned to repeat it. In my case, this meant that if I had ever bothered to study the history of malice I wouldn't have wasted the first forty-eight years of my life being malicious, as that was a dead-end street. So the first thing I decided to do after coming to terms with my own systemic deficiencies as a human being was to thoroughly acquaint myself with the history of goodness to see if I could pick up some pointers. By "goodness," I mean the conscious act of using all or most of one's intellectual and emotional resources to better both the human and the planetary condition, the way Jesus Christ and Florence

Nightingale and Mahatma Gandhi and Ben & Jerry had. In this sense "goodness" must be carefully distinguished from "niceness." Niceness is merely a set of cheerful attitudes that can be turned on and off at will. Goodness is a complete lifestyle. Down through the course of human history many a person has been stretched on the rack, beheaded, or crucified for being good. Nobody ever got executed for being nice.

With this distinction uppermost in my mind, I immersed myself in the copious and edifying literature of virtue.

Although Republicans hate to admit it, adults are a direct product of their youthful experiences, meaning that a child who grows up in a trailer park will be very different from a child who grows up in a house full of Bobby Short records. On this matter, I know whereof I speak. For although my parents strove valiantly to provide what they thought was a sane, nurturing environment while I was cutting my teeth on the mean streets of Philadelphia, it is clear that in certain areas they failed miserably.

Their most obvious deficiencies were in the area of personal growth, where my psyche was permanently ravaged by subpar spiritual mentoring, ultimately leaving me marooned on the high seas of the Baltimore Catechism. True, my parents raised me as a Roman Catholic, and true, they even encouraged me to pursue my dream of becoming a priest. But the fact that I dreamed of becoming a Maryknoll—known for their implacable martyrs—and not a Franciscan—known for their self-abnegation and piety—indicates that I was on the wrong track right from the start. As I look back on things, it is clear that at a very early age I misunderstood the central message of Christianity—love thine neighbor as thyself—and have gone through my life hamstrung by a fatally flawed belief system. This, not spitefulness, is why I grew up to be such a mean, horrible, and, in a very real sense, worthless person.

The reason my brand of Christianity is so defective lies perhaps in the fact that as a youth I chose all the wrong role models. Back in fifth grade, where I was press-ganged into serving as an altar boy at both the 5:30 A.M. and 6:30 A.M. masses *every day for an entire summer* at Raven Hill Academy, the smarmy private school where Grace Kelly acquired that weird, decidedly non–Keystone-state accent of hers, I was encouraged by the nuns to select a handful of upbeat, plausible role models from the Bible and *The Lives of the Saints* and use their values as a template in assembling my personality. To them, this meant zeroing in on stalwarts like my namesake Joseph of the Many-colored Coat, who had shown such clemency toward his treacherous brothers, or Saint Joseph, the father of Christ, a humble man known for his stolidity, lack of panache, and fine Galilean woodworking.

Nor was Joseph of Arimathaea, patron saint of morticians, entirely out of the running. Joseph, it will be recalled, is the trust-fund disciple who not only arranged for Christ's burial in the Arimathaea family crypt, but transported the Holy Grail to Glastonbury, England, where two millennia later Sting would perform at an outdoor concert evoking values similar to Christ's.

Other role models suggested to me were Saint Martin of Tours, the 3rd-century Roman cavalry officer who cut his cloak in half and gave it to an unidentified beggar; Saint Christopher, the apocryphal patron saint of messengers (though not of bike messengers); and Saint Anthony of Padua, the uncharacteristically chunky 13th-century holy man who is not actually remembered for anything in particular but who nevertheless managed to inspire hundreds, nay thousands, of tidy, terraced, carefully manicured backyard grottoes all over South Philadelphia.

None of these saints interested me. To a wide-eyed Irish-Catholic boy coming of age on the mean streets of Philadelphia in the late Eisenhower era, they seemed somehow too generic, too mundane, and in some cases, too Neapolitan. They cut few swaths, and those they did cut were not especially wide. No, the saints who caught my attention were the ones who had a little bit of swagger, just a *soupçon* of attitude, a smidgen of the old pizzazz.

The first luminary to appear on my radar screen was Saint Lawrence. Before he ran afoul of the authorities in A.D. 258, Lawrence was known as a harmless almsgiver. But one day the prefect of Rome ordered him to turn over the Church's wealth to the emperor Valerian, one of the true monsters of antiquity. Lawrence agreed to do so, but requested seventy-two hours to handle the paperwork. Three days later, the prefect became aware of a hubbub in the street, and peering out his window, lo and behold, there was Lawrence leading a crowd of lepers, beggars, cripples, widows, orphans, and ne'er-do-wells. This—Lawrence sneered—was the Church's wealth. The Empire was welcome to it.

The Romans, having put up with this kind of impudence from the Jews for centuries, were in no mood to be sassed by a parvenu Christian. So orders were given that Lawrence should be scourged, branded, stretched on the rack, and have his flesh ripped with sharp hooks before being roasted on a gridiron. Although his ordeal, by today's standards, seems quite barbarous, this type of punitive judicial procedure was par for the course in olden times, and would not automatically have made Lawrence a lock for Catholic Cooperstown.

No, what put Saint Lawrence over the top in the eyes of the hagiographic powers that be was a famous wisecrack he made to his tormentors in the midst of his agony. Bound to the gridiron and already roasted to a crisp, Lawrence was asked what he felt about his Lord and Savior now. Lawrence coolly replied: "I think I'm done on this side; you can turn me over now."

Yo' momma! Yes, to an impressionable tyke growing up on the mean streets of Philadelphia, this kind of in-your-face material was priceless. Lots of the early Christian martyrs had been flayed alive (Saint Bartholomew), broken on the wheel (Saint Catherine), deprived of their teeth (Saint Apollonia), crucified (Saint Peter, Saint Andrew), or fed to the lions (you name 'em). But there is no record of any of these individuals making a snappy comeback in the midst of their agony. Whether they lacked verbal ingenuity or were too caught up in the heat of the moment, none of the early Christian martyrs entered the history books by way of the sardonic put-down. Which is why a priceless jar of Saint Lawrence's sacred fat was shipped off as a gift to the Escorial in Spain by Pope Gregory XIII, and why the gridiron on which he was flame-broiled is still on display in the church of San Lorenzo in Rome.

As I worked my way through grade school, I thoroughly familiarized myself not only with the lives of the saints, but with the gruesome details of their deaths, always on the lookout for holy people who displayed a bit of a swagger when the Grim Reaper came a-knockin'. Saint Lucy, who, after being complimented by her pagan beau on her pretty eyes, gouged them out and handed them to him. Saint Perpetua, who after being tossed around by a wild heifer, grabbed the hand of her executioner and showed him how to slit her throat. Saint Phocas, who wined and dined the soldiers sent to murder him, and then, when they seemed too embarrassed to execute such a gracious host, reminded them that they would get into big trouble if they failed to do so. To top things off, Saint Phocas had even dug his own grave in the middle of the night while his executioners slept. Which is why he has long been revered as the patron saint of gravediggers, though, oddly enough, not of restaurateurs.

One thing I learned from reading these gruesome stories was that if you wanted to be remembered as a martyr, you really had to reach for the brass ring when the opportunity presented itself. When the shit hit the fan, you couldn't just sit back and let the heathen savages butcher you. You had to get right in their faces. You had to raise your game to another level. Yes, in the parlance of a later, more articulate era, you had to go for it.

Those who did not go for it have largely been consigned to the ash can of history. Because, let's face it, there is only so much material about torture and martyrdom that the average Catholic can assimilate at any one time. A good example is René Goupil, the very first of the North American martyrs. Goupil was captured by the Iroquois in 1642 and after the usual pavane of depravities (beating, skinning, scalding, hair and beard torn out, fingernails ripped out, fingers eaten or hacked off by his captors), he was dispatched by a tomahawk to the skull.

Pretty impressive, *n'est-ce pas*? Yet hardly anyone has ever heard of this otherwise remarkable man. The reason? He got completely upstaged by his companion Isaac Jogues, who went through exactly the same tortures, but survived them, and then managed to escape from the Indians, make his way back to France, and receive a special dispensation from the Pope to offer Mass with his stumps, before returning to the New World and dropping in on the very same folks who had mutilated him a year before. Then, and only then, did the Iroquois finally finish the job, planting a tomahawk in his skull, chopping off his head, and tossing his corpse into the river.

A wide-eyed youth, and still a bit of a pussy, I was totally blown away by Jogues's balls and bluster. For one, it showed that men armed with an unshakable faith in the Creator were not going to be discouraged by a bit of the rough stuff. But I also couldn't help wondering what the expressions on the faces of the Iroquois must have looked like when the missionary came strolling back into their camp, still intent on converting them, stumps and all, after all the unspeakable things they had done to him. What a slap in the face that must have been! Like: *Keep trying, guys. You'll get there.*

Although the reader may have already decided that at a very early age I had gone completely off the rails emotionally, a more careful review will make it clear why these martyrs so impressed me. For starters, these were men and women who didn't really have to work for a living, at least not in the nine-to-five sense. That would appeal to just about anyone. More to the point, they were people who obviously got off on giving complete strangers hell, secure in the knowledge that they occupied the moral high ground. Again, this would be of great appeal to a kid growing up in a housing project where you had to take a lot of crap from all and sundry. These were folks who loved to get into people's faces, pious wiseacres who always had to have the last laugh. To Little Joey Queenan, impoverished youth, this seemed like an absolutely fantastic career.

Obviously, I was not thrilled about the hatchets-in-the-penis or getting-my-forefingers-gnawed-off-by-squaws business. In fact, this is one of the main reasons I never became a priest. But another reason I did not become a priest was that somewhere along the line I realized that it was possible to participate in the upside of Christianity—the withering contempt for one's enemies, the ability to get in the last word—without having to participate in the downside (the fingernails torn out, the heart eaten, the red-hot pitch stuffed down the throat). I could do this by becoming a writer. I could grow up to be a satirist and lash the vice, not the man. I could be completely nasty to people I viewed as the Enemy, and get paid for it, without having to worry about being blinded or disemboweled.

Unfortunately, this is a road that ultimately leads nowhere. Sure, I grew up to be healthy and wealthy. But I did not grow up to be wise. And I most certainly did not grow up to be good. I am not saying that I grew up to be a mean person *entirely* because of my skewed interpretation of Christian history. Native Philadelphians are generally a pretty ghastly group of people, and the epic collapse of the 1964 Phillies only made things worse. I would only say that even by the standards of horrid Philadelphians—say my friends and family—I am viewed as an ungodly prick. So the first assignment I tackled after I began my search for spiritual self-regeneration was to go back and read up on the history of goodness, a story that I had never learned the first time around. Maybe this time I would get things right.

Although humanoid creatures have existed for hundreds of thousands of years, goodness per se is a relatively new concept. Crude paintings on cave walls such as those found in Africa, Australia, and southern France dating from 25,000 to 19,000 B.C. usually depict hunters killing large animals or small enemies, but there are no prehistoric visual records of any random acts of kindness carried out during man's embryonic era. More recently, a number of Mayan and Olmec vases produced around 1500 B.C. clearly depict humans handing objects to one another, but it is now believed that these acts were garden-variety commercial exchanges such as purchasing Incan myrrh on consignment, and not acts of pure altruism.

Paleophiles may argue that because recorded history does not begin until around 3000 B.C. it is impossible to say when mankind first manifested a capacity for goodness. Perhaps, they reason, the Neanderthals, the Druids, or even the Proto-Jutes were kind to each other but lacked the means to record it. This is a legitimate argument, but the facts strongly suggest otherwise. For what is most amazing about the history of virtue is how much time elapses between the first written records of any kind of human activity—hunting, farming, embalming—and the first written record of any specifically altruistic activity.

This happened around 1250 B.C., when the story of Noah was set down in the Bible. Although Noah probably did not exist, the very fact that anyone would even think of writing about a person as nice as him indicates that by 1250 B.C. the Hebrews were at least flirting with the concept of altruism. Up until then there is not a single mention of any human being ever doing anything truly kind to or for another human being. Historians agree that the Assyrians, the Hittites, the Hyksos, the Babylonians, the Chaldeans, the Medes, the Phrygians, and the Scythians were all vicious cocksuckers who contributed just about nothing to the amelioration of the human condition, while the Egyptians spent all their free time thinking about death.

Until the rise of Hebrew civilization the only human being in the history of mankind who ever did anything vaguely helpful for anybody was Hammurabi, the Babylonian king who codified, but did not actually create, the first system of laws known to mankind in about 1792 B.C. But Hammurabi's achievement, much like Napoleon Bonaparte's, was an administrative triumph, not a moral one. It made life easier, not better. The sad fact is, until Noah is first mentioned—1750 years after written history begins—there is no record of any human being behaving even as generously as, say, Jackson Browne. Of the storied peoples of antiquity, it is hard to think of a more scathing indictment. They simply did not know how to give back.

I am certainly not suggesting that there was never a good human being on the planet before Noah. I take it for granted that there have always been a few good souls: generous shepherds, benevolent blacksmiths, munificent farriers, stout yeomen. But these people were not famous, and famous good people are the only ones who interest us here. Why? Because it is the goodness of famous people that encourages ordinary people to also dare to be good. The world has always been blessed with upstanding basket weavers, ethical smelters, righteous glaziers. But because they were not famous, and because they were not ostentatious about their virtue, because they deliberately chose to hide their bushels beneath their baskets, yeah, verily, their fragrance was wasted on the desert air. Had they been just a bit more like Peter Gabriel, their names would to this very day hang from the lips of all humanity. And humanity would have been the better for their ostentation.

Anyway…Noah. Historians are not agreed as to whether Noah was an actual man or a composite figure fusing the deeds and personalities of numerous good men. But he was definitely the first man to realize that virtue practiced on the micro level was a waste of time, that if you wanted your deeds to resonate beyond the banks of the Tigris and the Euphrates, you had to do something spectacular, like saving the planet from a watery grave or warning unsuspecting consumers about the dangers posed by alar. Of course, Noah did have help from God.

After Noah, there are many Biblical figures who labored mightily both in the service of the Lord and of their fellow man. But unlike Noah or Jesus, figures who are the objects of almost universal veneration, most of these "good" people had a number of serious character flaws and thus served as poor role models for subsequent generations. Despite his obvious stature as a leader, Moses was the one who ordered the Levites to massacre the Hebrews who had worshiped the Golden Calf—and that was after the slaughter of the firstborn infants in Egypt. Shortly thereafter, Joshua stood by and did nothing while innocent women and children were massacred at the Battle of Jericho. These men may be heroes to the Chosen People, but they're not going to make any top ten list of moral exemplars in Egypt or most other parts of the Middle East.

Nor could the Biblical kings be described as paragons of virtue: Saul tried to kill David; David engineered the death of Uriah the Hittite; and Solomon was a skirt chaser par excellence. These men were certainly great, but it would be hard to describe them as good. Similarly, while history rings with the words of the great prophets—Samuel, Elijah, Isaiah, Ezekiel, Amos—who did not hesitate to upbraid the mighty for their iniquity—none of these people were especially likable. The prophets were Old Testament versions of Ralph Nader and Gore Vidal, bitchy scolds who kept a low profile for long periods of time before popping by to remind everyone how awful they were.

And such tempers! When the prophet Elisha was taunted about his baldness by a group of small children, he called forth two she-bears from the woods who promptly tore forty-two cheeky tykes to pieces. *Overkill Canyon.* For the most part, the only indisputably good people in the Old Testament are ordinary women like Esther and Susanna. But unlike Florence Nightingale or Susan Sarandon, these women are famous for doing one true thing when they were young and then resting on their laurels for the rest of their lives. Nightingale and Sarandon, in the patois of a later era, just kept on keeping on.

Did other civilizations produce certifiably good people during this period? No, most of the other civilizations of the ancient world came up completely empty in the goodness sweepstakes. Carthaginians? Dicks. Volscians? Bastards. Etruscans? *Schweinhunde*. Parthians? *Don't ask*. The obvious exception was the Greeks. After the Babylonian captivity, when the Chosen People started to run out of steam as a nation, the scepter of virtue passed to the Athenians, who produced two of the most famous good men the world has ever known. The first is Pericles, the mighty Athenian king, widely viewed as the Fiorello LaGuardia of his time. The second is Socrates, a man obsessed with placing the very best men in positions of power in the nation he loved. And that's not even mentioning such formidable second stringers as Galen, Hippocrates, Pythagoras, Protagoras, Euclid, and Diogenes.

Socrates is important not only because he was a good man but because he was, in the words of Bertrand Russell, somewhat "unctuous." Because of this aggressively unctuous quality, his fellow Athenians eventually tired of him and sentenced him to death. (Some historians contend that Socrates was killed because he was a corruptor of youth, but no, it was the unctuousness that did him in.) Indeed, Socrates was the first man in history to have his life ended because of unctuousness, but he would not be the last. Unctuousness was also responsible for the deaths of Saint Paul and many of the early Christian saints, and may have contributed to the early demises of Howard Cosell and Sammy Davis Jr. Virtue combined with unctuousness would not make an effective combination until the rise of Jimmy Carter, some 2400 years after Socrates swallowed the hemlock. It is also worth noting that Socrates was physically quite unattractive, and was the first virtuous bad dresser in history, inaugurating twin traditions that would continue straight through with John the Baptist, Saint Jerome, Saint Francis of Assisi, and Ben & Jerry.

From the death of Socrates, in 399 B.C., until the birth of Christ, in A.D. 9, good people either ceased to exist or kept a very low profile. This is because there were so many nations vying for power in the same general geographical region that it was impossible for good people to flourish. The forward-minded Gracchi Brothers had a brief fling in Rome in the second century B.C., but were assassinated before they could get their Tiber Valley Rainbow Coalition off the ground. Everyone else who tried to improve the condition of the common man met a similar fate. After the Republic collapsed when Julius Caesar crossed the Rubicon in 49 B.C., the Romans didn't even try to produce any good men, as there was no money in it. By the time Christ was born, late in the reign of Augustus, there were but a handful of good people left on the face of the earth—a few seers, one or two iron smelters, several mysterious virgins—but none of them were public figures, so we can ignore them.

Yet within a century of Christ's death, the world was literally crawling with good people. The crucifixion triggered an explosion of public virtue that was not to be repeated in human history until the late 20th century, when such varied figures as Susan Sarandon, Ben & Jerry, Barbra Streisand, Tom Cruise, Bono, Kim Basinger, Whoopi Goldberg, Alec Baldwin, Don Henley, and Sting would collectively do as much good for humanity in a decade or so as the early Christians did in almost three centuries.

One reason Whoopi, Sting, and Susan have been more efficient than the early Christians is because they have had a much longer shelf life. As opposed to Jesus Himself, who seems to have genuinely enjoyed a nice meal, a bit of chitchat, the company of friends, most of the early Christians led their lives as if they had a bus to catch. By and large, they couldn't wait to be broken on the wheel, fed to lions, crucified. And, as the story of Saint Lawrence make clear, the Romans were ultimately powerless before a cult of people who thought life was a big joke and went out of their way to get murdered.

Historians have long debated why so many of the early Christians deliberately antagonized their tormentors into tying their entrails to a windlass and then letting 'er rip. Was it because they had been promised that the freshly martyred would immediately be ushered into the presence of the Lord? Or was a bit of grandstanding going on? The truth is a mixture of the two. As the martyrs grew in number, it became much more difficult to attract attention by having your entrails tied to a windlass and ripped out. By A.D. 300, martyrdom had become such a common event that blasé hagiographers did not even bother themselves about little details like that anymore.

Thus, we do not know whether Saint Agnes was burned, stabbed, or decapitated, and we also do not know whether her suitor Eutropius was blinded or struck dead when he tried to defile her. To better understand why so many Christians went out of their way to be martyred in a particularly horrible fashion at a time that the public was starting to lose interest in such extravagant behavior, consider the following analogy. In 1979 Ken Dryden led the National Hockey League with a 2.30 Goals Against average. Yet, had Dryden still been tending goal in 1999, he would have finished fourteenth, far behind Dominik Hasek, Martin Brodeur, and Ron Tugnutt. It is much the same with the great saints. Saint Teresa of Avila (1515–1582), who never came close to being martyred, is revered because she lived in an era when the standards of virtue were so low that merely having the Seven Wounds of Christ could make you famous. Had she lived in the time of Saint Lucy, when you had to pop your eyes out of their sockets to get attention, Teresa and her dainty stigmata would have been laughed right out of the Roman Empire.

Indeed, in studying the lives of the saints and the fathers of the church, one senses that they were engaged in a high-stakes poker game to see who could endure the most abuse, thus achieving the greatest sanctity—and immortality.

Saint Agatha: I'll fast my entire life, carve scars in my face, and sleep on a bed of rusty nails.

Origen: See you and raise you. I'll wear a belt of nails that will rip my flesh, carve my face up with a knife, wash the floor with my tongue, fast my entire life, and go live in the desert among the wild beasts.

Saint Sernin: See and raise, but I'll also get tied to the tail of a bull and dragged around the city until my brains shoot out through my eardrums.

Saint Margaret: Too rich for my blood.

Saint Agatha: There's a time to hold 'em and a time to fold 'em.

Origen: I'll get dragged around until my brains explode through my eardrums, drink mucus from a dying leper's breasts, and cut off my penis.

Saint Sernin: I fold.

Another reason the number of martyrdoms declined so sharply after the 3rd century is that so many political and judicial figures involved in the murder of the saints came to a bad end. Two years after Valerian ordered the barbecuing of Saint Lawrence, he was captured by the Persians and flayed alive. At roughly the same time, Saint Barbara's father Dioscurus became so incensed with his daughter's refusal to renounce her faith that he turned her over to the authorities, who flogged her, broke her bones, and cut off her breasts. When this failed to make an impression, Dioscurus chopped off her head, only to be promptly struck dead by lightning.

For both procedural and stylistic reasons, the Romans finally converted to Christianity, as it was the only way to induce people to concentrate on their work and not spend all their time trying to get the authorities mad enough to flay them alive and feed their entrails to roving jackals. For a short time, Christians took solace from their triumph, beguiling themselves into thinking that they had established the kingdom of heaven on earth. But ultimately, because of its credo that life on this planet was a dreary prelude to the rapture waiting in Paradise, the triumph of Christianity led to the collapse of the Roman Empire, and this set back the cause of virtue almost a thousand years.

After the last Roman emperor was deposed in A.D. 476, public goodness ceased to exist in the ancient world. Good people went into hiding and stayed there. The Christians hid from the Lombards, the Visigoths, the Huns, the Jutes. The Arabs hid from the Persians. The Persians hid from the Mongols. And the Jews hid from everybody. You could count on your fingers the number of good people still extant—a few monks, some Jewish mystics, two Arab philosophers—and they certainly didn't accomplish much. Almost all of the energies of good people went into preserving the great treasures of the past and waiting for the Dark Ages to blow over so that civilized people could get out of Ireland and go back to some interesting place, like France. Unfortunately, the Dark Ages didn't blow over for seven hundred years.

Modern virtue begins with Saint Francis of Assisi (1182–1226), who not only did not get himself martyred, but did not seem to feel that it would reflect badly on him if he didn't. Born into the rag trade,

Francis originally seemed destined for a military career. But one day he spotted a leper and impetuously jumped off his horse and kissed him. This was not as unusual an act as it might seem today. Physical interaction with lepers has long been a fixture in the culture of virtue; from the time Jesus healed a leper in A.D. 32 to the time the Belgian cleric Father Damien went to live with lepers on the island of Molokai in 1864, leprosy played the same role in Western civilization as the rain forest does today. That is, if you wanted to get the word out what a virtuous person you were, you either kissed a leper, bathed a leper, drank the pus from a leper's breasts, or invited a leper over to the house to play draughts. Had Ben & Jerry been alive a few centuries ago, they would surely have marketed a flavor called Leper Crunch or Maraschino Molokai.

Obviously, Saint Francis did a lot more than kiss lepers. Had he merely kissed a leper, or even a series of lepers, he would quickly have faded from the pages of history. No, Saint Francis's greatest achievement was that he managed to be a good person without being incredibly annoying. This had never happened before in all of human history. Socrates, as noted, was unctuous. The early Christian martyrs had a bit of the hot dog in them. And while it is true that Christ's contemporaries liked him, He could definitely get on people's nerves with his constant bellyaching about the Pharisees, the Saducees, His Father leaving Him high and dry, etc. Not Saint Francis.

Historically, Saint Francis is important for three other reasons. One, he was the father of environmentalism, the first person who believed that animals were at least as important as human beings, and usually much better company. Two, he was the first person in history to prove that it was possible to be good and still have a lot of fun. Were not his dying words, "Hey, we got any of that marzipan left?" Three, he revived the ancient tradition established by Noah of practicing ostentatious virtue, and making sure that everyone knew what a fantastic person he was. In this sense, he is the spiritual antecedent of Ted Turner.

As the Renaissance and the Reformation gathered steam, Europe witnessed the rise of the secularly virtuous; that is, people whose goodness had no specific religious connotation and who were not interested in being martyrs or socializing with lepers. In this class may be included many great scientists. But not all, and probably not most. For although scientists and inventors have contributed a disproportionate amount to the amelioration of the human condition, a large number of them have been scoundrels, often receiving enormous "stipends" and stock options for their work. And very few of them could actually be described as "nice." Moreover, because scientists are so much smarter than ordinary human beings, they make poor role models. Anyone can grow up to start a socially conscious premium ice-cream company in Vermont. But it takes real smarts to discover a cure for cholera.

There is another reason for putting scientists in a category separate from the indisputably good. Many of the most famous scientists were vivisectionists. Louis Pasteur's rival Claude Bernard conducted experiments so grisly that his wife and children refused to have anything more to do with him. Emil Roux, Pasteur's devoted disciple, used to paralyze rabbits with what Paul de Kruif, author of *Microbe Hunters,* referred to as "diptheria soup." Elie Metchnikoff, trailblazing venerealist, once infected a healthy ape with syphilis, then cut off its ear. Lazzaro Spallanzani, who proved that microbes carry disease, would sever a male toad's legs while it was copulating with a female toad, just to see how it would react. So, whatever their longtime services to mankind, many of our greatest scientists were amoral sadists who do not deserve to be mentioned in the same breath as Jesus, Saint Francis of Assisi or Tom of Maine.

One need only contrast the philosophy of Louis Pasteur with that of Tom of Maine to see how morally deficient the great scientists of the past have been. Pasteur was an arrogant, bigoted, chauvinistic egomaniac who put his lab animals through hell. In one experiment, he let his assistants drill a hole into a dog's skull and drip dangerous microbes directly on its brain. Tom of Maine would never do anything like that; Kate of Maine wouldn't let him. And although the argument can be made that organic toothpaste is less important to humanity than a cure for tuberculosis, Tom's influence as a person is greater because he managed to help mankind without hurting rats, the lowest of the animals. In the long run, I believe, Tom of Maine will be remembered long after Pasteur of Paree has been forgotten.

Once scientists are eliminated from the roster of the virtuous, the

pickings are pretty slim. Indeed, between the death of Saint Francis of
Assisi in 1226 and the birth of Johnny Appleseed in 1775, there are no
famous ordinary good people in the annals of history. Appleseed,
whose real name was John Chapman, was born in Leominster,
Massachusetts. From a very early age, he devoted his life to planting
apple trees, encouraging others to do so, and making sure that everyone knew he was doing it. What's more, he did all this barefoot. A lovable ditz who was constantly accompanied by a mangy wolf and was
respected by the Indians, Appleseed once found himself alone in the
wilderness in the dead of winter and built a fire at one end of a hollow
log. Suddenly, he heard a frightened sound from inside the log, where
he discovered a terrified mother and cub. So he put out the fire and slept
the entire night in the snow. Obviously, since no one was on hand to
corroborate this incident, it is possible that Appleseed may have invented or embellished this story, just as Ben & Jerry may be exaggerating
when they claim to have learned how to make the people's ice cream by
taking a $5 correspondence course from Penn State. But as Appleseed
spent his life wearing a saucepan backwards as a hat, it certainly seems
like the sort of thing he would do, so there is no reason to doubt him.

One possible explanation for the paucity of good people in the
past is that it used to be hard to be a good person and have a career at
the same time, and rich people were too busy being evil. Moreover, history is filled with examples of gentle souls who went out of their way
to help their fellow man but whose philanthropy actually ended up
making a bad situation worse. Saint Bernard of Clairvaux (1090–1153)
was reputed to be one of the world's great conciliators, a beloved sage
who would travel any distance to bring about peace between warring
parties. Yet Saint Bernard is responsible for the Crusades, one of the
most repellent episodes in history, which resulted not only in the massacre of Muslims and Jews, but in the sack of Constantinople.

This is not the only example of the Law of Unintended Effects. In
1682, William Penn, a devout English Quaker, set out to establish a
heaven on earth in the New World. Instead, he founded Philadelphia.

Earlier in the same century Squanto, a member of the now extinct Patuxet tribe, taught the Pilgrims how to grow corn. This was a wonderful, selfless act. But because Squanto's act of generosity enabled the perfidious white man to get a foothold in North America, thus setting in motion the cycle that would lead to the death of the buffalo, the Trail of Tears, the massacre at Wounded Knee, and *Dances with Wolves*, his virtue was not an unqualified success. Sacagawea and Black Kettle fall into the same category: swell folks who simply backed the wrong horse.

By the 19th century, people were beginning to recognize that human goodness without a solid bureaucratic infrastructure was basically a waste of time. Though a few individuals managed to flourish in relative isolation (Dr. Livingstone, Father Damien, Robert Owen, Louis Braille, Louisa May Alcott), the 19th century was essentially an age of institutional virtue. Former slave Harriet Tubman established the Underground Railroad, which carried so many of her fellow African Americans to freedom, but she had lots of help. Florence Nightingale literally created the profession of nursing in the mid-19th century, but she was not alone. William Booth founded the Salvation Army in 1878, Clara "The Angel of the Battlefield" Barton founded the American branch of the Red Cross in 1881, and eight years later, uber-social worker Jane Addams founded Hull House in Chicago. But unlike Jesus, they had lots of financial backing, and rarely worked alone.

This leads us to the 20th century, where no list of good people would be complete without such names as Nelson Mandela, Mother Teresa, Albert Schweitzer, Mahatma Gandhi, Desmond Tutu, Kim Basinger, and various Dalai Lamas. Ironically, because the 20th century has been so awful, there have been many more opportunities for extraordinary human beings to show their goodness. Raoul Wallenberg, a Swedish businessman and diplomat, risked life and limb to save 100,000 Hungarian Jews from the Nazis. Oscar Schindler did similar good deeds for the Jews of Poland. Martin Luther King, Medger Evers, and Malcolm X all got themselves assassinated while gallantly trying to advance the cause of their people. And Sting raised public consciousness by writing that song about the *desaparecidos* of Chile. Or maybe it was Argentina. Anyway, somewhere in South America.

But the most important development in 20th-century virtue, particularly in the years since the Second World War, has been the rise of accessible role models. Very few people alive today would have the stomach to put up with the kind of nonsense that Jesus and Gandhi had to endure. But Michael Stipe's daily roster of events doesn't seem so bad. Whereas the Early Christians got sent to the hospital, Princess Di opened hospitals. In essence, our latter-day saints have learned how to be good without being gross, and have also learned how to practice virtue without getting taken to the cleaners financially. In the words of Ben & Jerry, "If it's not fun, why do it?"

Fun aside, there are vast psychological rewards to be derived from practicing virtue at the dawn of the new millennium. One of the best things about being an altruistic person in the age of MSNBC is that one's good deeds are not likely to be forgotten. Saint Margaret, one of the virgin martyrs, was supposedly eaten by a dragon and then beheaded during the reign of Diocletian, thus becoming one of the most popular saints in medieval Europe. Yet historians and even certain hagiographers now debate whether she ever existed. Another female saint supposedly forded the Rhine on the back of a giant sturgeon to escape from the roaming palms of Charlemagne, but for the life of me I can't even remember her name. By contrast, we know that Whoopi Goldberg and Robin Williams hosted *Comic Relief IV*, that Jimmy Carter hammered nails into the roofs of low-income houses in the South Bronx, and that Jackson Browne has given concerts to support shade-grown coffee—and no future generation will ever be able to dispute that.

One caveat. In reviewing the history of goodness, it is important to distinguish between actions that are motivated by a genuine love of humanity and good deeds carried out to salve one's conscience or for public relations purposes. The Rockefellers, the Carnegies, the Morgans, and their modern counterparts have all done wonderful things for the public, but they only did them in an effort to camouflage the fact that they were basically scum-sucking pigs. By contrast, Johnny Appleseed planted trees all over the Midwest because he genuinely loved humanity and genuinely loved trees, and the same can be said of Bette Midler, who once adopted part of a highway and has been very active in the Gotham community-garden scene. As a rule of thumb, if a person has a wing dedicated to him at a major metropolitan art museum, it's a safe bet that he is or was an evil person. Johnny Appleseed, Bette Midler, and Susan Sarandon do not. So draw your own conclusions.

Through my survey of virtue down through the ages, I finally came to understand that a person did not have to be a confrontational prick in order to improve the human condition. Moreover, I now recognized that the *carte blanche* cruelty that I had practiced over my long career as a satirist was little more than a smoke screen to disguise a genuinely malignant personality. I pretended that I was being cruel because that was what satirists did for a living. But the truth of the matter was, I enjoyed being mean.

Happily, my study of history had introduced me to the redemptive power of contrition. I could take comfort in the fact that one's past misanthropy need not be a millstone around one's neck, much less an albatross, also around one's neck. History abounded with stories of good men and women who had been quite capable of unspeakable behavior before their penitent feet finally carried them into the presence of the Lord. Moses slew a man in anger, but made up for it by leading the Israelites out of Egypt. Solomon screwed everything that moved, but repented by building the Temple. Jimmy Carter single-handedly wrecked the American economy, but atoned for it by hammering nails into the roofs of low-income houses in the South Bronx. And Don Henley wrote "The Best of Your Love," but wiped out this blot on the moral ledger by raising money to save Walden Wood. All of which demonstrated that it was never too late to turn over a new leaf, to straighten up and fly right. And if it was not too late for these people, it certainly was not too late for me. Yes, I was ready to start a new life. The Good Life.

And I was ready to start it now.

4 • Today Is the

First Day of the

Rest of Your Life

ow that I had steeped myself in the lore of virtue, I prepared to set out on the Golden Road to Unlimited Devotion. How does a mean, uncaring, fundamentally bad person suddenly turn his life around? For starters, by getting the infrastructure of virtue in place. The right clothing (no fur, no alligator-skin shoes). The right books (*The Gita*, the *I Ching*, Ben & Jerry's *Double-Dip*). The right food (Newman's Own, various tofu-based meat substitutes), the right beverages (Edensoy, kefir, shade-grown coffee). And yes, even the right toiletries. That's why the first stop on my first shopping expedition as a recovering horrible human being was the Body Shop.

My, oh my, did I go on a spree! First, some aromatic soaps—grape, watermelon, lime, star fruit, pink grapefruit, satsuma—which set me back ten bucks. Then some deodorant, sun lotion, facial sun stick, and shaving cream that clipped another double sawbuck off my bankroll. Despite these hefty price tags, the merchandise had a subliminal ethical allure because each item carried a notice indicating that no animals had been tested during the development of the products. So before you knew it, I had loaded up with the star fruit lip balm, the rice bran body scrub, the aromatic body bar, the jasmine bath "fizzy," and even the Seaweed and Peony shampoo. Finally, just for good measure, I grabbed a beach towel adorned with a photograph of a chunky toy doll, upon which had been superimposed the message, "There are three billion women who don't look like supermodels and only eight who do." Presumably, Anita Roddick, founder of the Body Shop, was not among the eight. I applied for a Body Shop Discount Card, then watched as the salesperson loaded my merchandise into a shopping bag that read

IF YOU THINK EDUCATION IS EXPENSIVE, TRY IGNORANCE

Tell me about it. I *had* tried ignorance. And was that ever a dead end.

Before embarking on my program of spiritual self-renewal, I could honestly say that I had never set foot in a Body Shop before, not even to make fun of it. Sure, I knew the whole Body Shop mythology about Anita Roddick founding a company that would combine humane treatment of personnel with humane treatment of animals—because I'd ridiculed that concept in a magazine article several years before— but up until now I thought it was just a spiel. Now that I'd spent six weeks researching the history of virtue, I'd come across a couple of publications that completely changed my mind about this.

One was *Shopping for a Better World*, published by the Council on Economic Priorities. The guide, almost four hundred pages long, rated some two thousand products by more than two hundred companies according to various ethical criteria. Each product was listed in a column on the left-hand side, and next to it were tiny boxes rating the manufacturer's track record vis-a-vis the environment, charitable giving, community outreach, women's advancement, minority advancement, family, workplace issues, and disclosure of information. On the right-hand side was a box informing the shopper about related issues, such as whether the firm conducted animal testing or was engaged in the man-ufacture of military weapons. Consumers were encouraged to carry the guide with them whenever they went shopping, though this was not terribly practical, as the book was roughly the size of *The Complete Works of Anna Quindlen*.

Frankly, I was disappointed at how cumbersome the guide was, because I had complained about the graphics and layout of the original shopping guide in *Forbes* ten years earlier, when I was still an unenlight-ened person. At the time, I reported that *Shopping for a Better World* was so complicated and blighted by such hideous graphics that it would take an eternity for a good person to figure out which products to buy. As I noted, "what the Council on Economic Priorities has inadvertently done is to put together a guide that really benefits morally degenerate consumers. Because it flags corporate miscreants in its 'Alert' box…a moral leper could be in and out of the supermarket in five minutes flat."

Today, I was ashamed of having taken such a vicious cheap shot and was ready to give *Shopping for a Better World* a second chance. Well, I have to admit, I still had problems with the little devil. Because my eyes had given out long ago and my concentration was shot, it was impossible for me to keep straight whether the graphic depicting a handshake symbolized support for "same-sex relationships," "commu-nity outreach," or "takes bribes," so there was no way I was taking the guide with me every single time I went to market. In fact, the first time I took it on a road test—when I went shopping for guitar strings—I dis-covered that the guide had no listing for the product or manufacturer, so it was impossible to determine whether the merchandise had been torn from a cat's entrails or a mountain goat's esophagus or was entire-ly synthetic. It was equally obvious that a manual such as this would be no use in the purchase of exotic products such as kayak grommets or crotchless panties or carburetors, and thus could be mocked by cynics for its extremely constricted vista.

But I was no longer one of those cynics. This time around I would have no truck with intellectually threadbare sophistries, even though they had been my stock in trade for years. No, in my new frame of mind, I recognized that most of the ordinary products (detergents, shampoos, beverages, canned goods) that ordinary people (gays, minorities, the deaf, the blind, Native Americans, Special Olympics children, white people) used in their households in their everyday lives were included in the shopping guide, and for them the guide could be very useful indeed. The key here was to use the manual to evaluate everything I owned, eliminate all morally unacceptable products, and then restock the house with suitable replacements.

Since cleanliness was next to godliness, and godliness was what I was after, I started with the bathroom. This took me about three weeks, because Operation Purge the John had to be carried out surreptitiously. Even though my wife is deeply concerned about the fate of the earth and gives money to Greenpeace and MADD and Amnesty International, she's English and therefore stingy. For example, if I'd told her that we could no longer use a particular brand of shampoo because the manufacturer was conducting cruel experiments on the people who lived down the street, she would have said, "I'll remember not to buy it anymore, but let's use up what we already have."

This being the case, whenever my wife was away from home, I'd sneak into our bathroom and check to see if the products we were using were morally abhorrent. If they were, I'd toss them into the trash, hoping that she wouldn't notice. This clandestine operation was not easy—and not just because I had trouble reading the graphics. The fact is, I was already suffering from information overload and had a hard time making up my mind how bad a company had to be before I could bring myself to give its products the old heave-ho. For example, I used to love one particular shampoo because it had an almost magical ability to maintain the luster in my disintegrating hair and was always on sale at CVS. But now The Council on Economic Priorities was telling me that the company routinely tested on animals, had a poor record with regard to female employees, and wasn't doing anything special for minorities or, as far as I could see, minority hair. Much as I loved the way my hair looked after using this fine product (full body, perky sheen, no tangles), there was no way I could continue buying it under these circumstances.

But where was I to turn for an acceptable replacement? According to the CEP one company had deficient family policies, another had an uninspiring record on minority advancement, and a third conducted animal testing. The situation resolved itself fortuitously, thanks to Tom of Maine. One day, while rereading all that information on the back of my toothpaste container, I decided to send away for *Personal Care for People Who Care: A Guide to Choosing Cruelty-free Cosmetics, Household and Personal-care Products.* This was a manual published by the National Anti-Vivisection Society, and it listed all of the companies that conducted tests on animals. This made things a whole lot easier on me, because the companies included the manufacturers of virtually every product in my bathroom. Now I could simply slash and burn; rather than asking myself whether I should keep the cough medicine despite the company's stinginess toward charities, or throw out the cotton swabs because the company had a sexist policy toward women, I simply loaded up a 30-gallon trash bag and threw out everything in the bathroom. And then I went to the Body Shop, where there simply is no moral confusion.

All told, I tossed out eleven bottles of shampoo, thirty-seven bars of soap, eleven tubes of bath gel, six jars of hair conditioner, five cans of shaving cream, thirty-five disposable razors, and around twenty-three bottles of home medications. The purge nicked around $300 from my bankroll, not exactly chump change. I didn't care that much about the money, but the one thing that did annoy me was that I had to chuck out all those pint-sized complimentary containers of shampoo and soap and bath gel and conditioner that I'd filched from hotels all over the planet. These items rarely carried the name of the manufacturer, but as I had found them in hotels that catered to businessmen, I had to assume that they were made by companies that mistreated gays, castrated cocker spaniels, and used the "N" word when African-Americans were out of the room. Or, in the case of the six jars of shampoo I'd heisted from the Quay West Hotel in Sydney, Australia, African-Australians. In any case, I knew that I had to do the right thing here. Heave-ho.

. . .

My purchases at the Body Shop had come to $93.71, all of which went on my credit card. My new credit card. My Amnesty International Platinum Plus credit card, which I signed up for after spotting an ad in *Mother Jones*. This classy, attention-getting card had a number of advantages: It carried no annual fee and offered a low introductory 3.9 percent APR on cash-advance checks, but the best news was that the bank issuing the card would make a donation to Amnesty International each time I made a purchase. Ironically, this meant that if I used the card to book a vacation in Baghdad, Saddam Hussein would inadvertently be funding an organization that was implacably opposed to his regime. Such were the ironies of the modern world. Tee-hee.

Next I decided that I must do something about my morally neutral checkbook. For years I had been paying my bills with innocuous baby blue checks issued by that hulking monolith Citibank. But one day, again while perusing *Mother Jones,* I spied an ad for a St. Paul, Minnesota, firm called Message!Products. Message!Products had been founded in 1985 by a forward-looking woman who believed that Message!Checks would be a great way for people to show what they cared about by having their personal checks adorned with various slogans. It was also a mechanism for various worthy organizations to raise money for their political, cultural, philosophical, vegetarial, homoerotic, gynecological, aquatic, sapphic, pachydermal, avian, amphibian, prenatal or African-American causes. According to the organization's website, Message!Checks had already raised $250,000 for a plethora of causes. Pretty impressive, indeed.

The elegant checks (printed on recycled paper with soy-based inks) sold for $13.95 (plus $3.95 shipping and handling) and could be ordered in snazzy checkbooks complete with covers made of sturdy hemp. The merchandise depicted in *Mother Jones* came in four styles: a somewhat garish golden check with the words PRO-CHOICE emblazoned across it, a bland yellow check which indicated support for House Resolution AS910 (human rights), a bright white check with an adorable photo of an affable kitten and what appeared to be a guinea pig beneath the message STOP ANIMAL TESTING, and a green-and-white check sporting the Greenpeace symbol.

For a number of reasons, none of these motifs was quite what I was looking for. Because I had been raised as a Catholic and still vaguely believed in God, and in fact still vaguely believed in an omnipotent and vengeful God, I opted to steer clear of the pro-choice checks, because if God did exist, I had reason to believe that He probably took more of a pro-life stance on this issue than most *Mother Jones* readers, and I didn't want to alienate Him.

There was also the question of sensitivity: Most of the checks I write go to my mother (a devout Catholic) and my landlord (a Muslim). At this late date in her life, I wasn't going to risk offending my mother by forcing her into the morally indefensible position of cashing a check that would help to foster the cause of the abortion movement. Although I did not actually believe that requiring my mother to cash a check with the words PRO-CHOICE on it would get her excommunicated from the Church or anything, I suspected that *she* did. As for my landlord, I had no idea what the Islamic stand on abortion was, but after that Salman Rushdie dust-up, I never, ever risked upsetting Muslims. So these controversial items got the thumbs-down.

The other selections were a bit problematic as well. The human-rights check was astoundingly nondescript, but, more to the point, it seemed to me that saying you supported human rights was kind of namby-pamby, like saying you were in favor of motherhood or were implacably opposed to Nazism. The Greenpeace check was a tad generic, and since my wife already contributed to that organization anyway, it seemed a waste to double up on my support. As for the stop-animal-testing check, well, frankly, it was just a bit too cutesy for a gnarled old curmudgeon like me. When I'd planted my feet on the road to redemption, I was consciously modeling myself after tough customers like Jesus Christ, Mahatma Gandhi, and Martin Luther King. Frankly, I was not interested in turning into some kind of eco-wuss. Also, I don't actually like cats or rodents.

But more important, I figured that if I was going to start wearing my heart on my checks, I should choose something with a bit more *oomph*. So, one afternoon I called the Message!Checks people at their headquarters in St. Paul and asked if I could get something more colorful and personal.

"Just out of curiosity, how many check designs do you have?" I asked the socially conscious sales rep when she picked up the phone.

"We now have slogans from over one hundred organizations," she told me.

"I was wondering if it was possible to design my own checks?" I inquired. "I have a few ideas in mind."

"No, I'm sorry, we don't do that," she replied.

"Oh," I said, crestfallen. "Well, let me ask you, do you have any checks with the slogan *Una Puebla Unida Jamas Sera Vencida*? That's always been one of my favorites from back in the movement days."

"No, I'm sorry, we don't," she answered. Oddly, it did not seem like this was the first time she had been asked this question. Not by a long shot. Disappointed but determined to find something a bit more riveting, I hung up and then logged on to the company's website and started checking out some of the other options available to me. It soon became obvious that Message!Products had their bases pretty well covered, with categories such as Animal, Environmental, Social, and the all-purpose More Issues. There were also plain checks under the heading Classic Conscience, which definitely caught my fancy. But in the end I decided on the Breast-feeding Checks, which helped raise money for the La Leche League. I chose these simple but elegant checks, which depicted a woman nursing her baby, because I honestly believe that breast-fed babies grow up to be better human beings than bottle-fed babies, and bottle-fed babies grow up to be worse than breast-fed babies, as witnessed by the fact that I had not been breast-fed. So sending those garish checks to my mother was a nice way to get a bit of good-natured geriatric ribbing in. While making an important social point.

With the credit card and the Message!Checks on the way, I had made a good start in getting the financial underpinnings of my new lifestyle in place. The next item on the agenda involved switching my long-distance phone carrier from the amoral MCI to Working Assets Long Distance. Here I could kill two—perhaps three—birds with one stone (if such an ecologically insensitive remark can be allowed). The great advantage of switching to Working Assets Long Distance was that it was "the leading long distance company working for peace, human rights, equality, education and the environment." Moreover, Working Assets claimed that its rates were cheaper than those of its vile competitors.

But that wasn't all. No, what made this long-distance phone service so attractive at this juncture in my life was the knowledge that Working Assets would donate 1 percent of my long-distance charges to progressive nonprofits such as Friends of the Earth, the Natural Resources Defense Council, the National Association for the Advancement of Colored People, and Fairness & Accuracy in Reporting, an organization I had previously ridiculed in *Time*. This meant that on days when I was too busy or tired to support social causes in a demonstrative fashion, I could passively help better the human condition by simply making a few long-distance phone calls.

You would have thought this would have been enough. But no, there was more. Every month, my phone bill would alert me to two critical issues that Working Assets had designated of the utmost importance. If it turned out that these issues also concerned me, Working Assets would let me telephone the targeted leaders free every day of the week (up to two calls a day, five minutes in length.) I was also very impressed to learn that my bill would be printed on 100 percent post-consumer recycled paper printed with soy ink. (By this point, I was starting to realize that soy was going to be a much more important legume in my life in the future than it had ever been in the past.) Last but not least, Working Assets would give me sixty free minutes of long-distance calls every month for the next six months plus a pint of Ben & Jerry's ice cream every month for a year. They had made me an offer I could not possibly refuse.

Until this point in my life, I had been the sort of person who didn't return phone calls to people who lived in other states, preferring to let them pay for the call. But now I was ready to alter my policy, cheerfully making expensive long-distance calls, safe in the knowledge that each call I made would help to advance the cause of social justice somehow, somewhere.

There was only one thing that bothered me about this arrangement. Most of my friends were wishy-washy liberals, so calling them would dovetail nicely with the spirit of social activism fostered by Working Assets. But what about when I called my more conservative friends, such as Andy Ferguson, the aforementioned former George Bush speechwriter and columnist for Rupert Murdoch's *Weekly Standard* and therefore a tool of Satan? Wasn't I guilty of fiber-optic hypocrisy in calling him in his right-wing Washington office over a phone line based in liberal San Francisco? Similarly, wasn't it immoral to use a Greenpeace credit card to pay for things like tuna fish or gasoline?

Little by little over the course of the next few weeks, this situation became truly distressing. Every time I would reach for the phone to call Andy or any of my other right-wing, and, in some cases, ultra–right-wing, friends, I would feel the remorseless gaze of my morally rejuvenated telephone receiver glaring back at me. *"Phony." "Hypocrite." "Fascist."* It seemed to taunt me. Sure, there was a part of me that consoled myself with the thought that I was engaging in outright subversion by keeping right-wing people on the phone for long conversations and thus inadvertently tricking them into helping me to advance the causes they most despised. Justice. Equality. Human Rights. The Rain Forest. But in the end I realized that I was only fooling myself. In the end, I decided to make all my right-wing calls from a pay phone, thus preserving the moral inviolability of the receiver in my office. But in the back of my mind I was already gravitating toward an important decision to never call any of these "friends" again, as they were basically very bad people.

For the next few days, I basked in the sunshine of my newfound love of humanity. But every time I thought that I had all the bases covered, I discovered some other lifestyle deficiency. Take haberdashery. Like most people of my general age and ilk, my massive T-shirt collection consisted entirely of sports themes (Philadelphia 76ers, Phillies, Eagles, and Flyers) and garish items fraught with irony *(Bobby Vinton: Branson; John Tesh: The Concert for Avalon; Cats)*. Now it was time for a complete change. Following a chain of Internet links from a socially conscious organization I found in the classifieds section of *Mother Jones,* I made my way to a website run by the the No.H.A.R.M. (Northampton

Human and Animal Rights Movement) Store in Northampton, Massachusetts. No.H.A.R.M. was a retail establishment existing only in compassionate cyberspace that provided people like me with the opportunity to purchase cruelty-free and socially conscious T-shirts as well as bumper stickers and buttons.

There were quite a number of T-shirts to choose from, including such wiseacre classics as "Boycott Homophobia," "Columbus Did Not Discover the New World, He Invaded It," "Arm Bears," and "Lobotomies for Republicans," but I decided to stick with more traditional favorites such as "It Takes a Whole Village...to Raise a Child," "Defend the Earth," "Honor Diversity," and, of course, "Practice Random Kindness and Senseless Acts of Beauty" because I believed that wearing these shirts would help me to bond with like-minded people whom I had until now despised.

Next, I started making my selections from the enormous number of bumper stickers offered by No.H.A.R.M. for two bucks apiece. From the Animal Rights and Vegetarianism section I narrowed it down to "Animals Don't Drink, Smoke, or Use Drugs, Except in Labs," "Rats Have Rights," "Remember the Elephants...Forget Ivory," "Fur Is Dead," and "I Don't Eat Anything with a Face." From the Feminism and Women's Issues section I picked "If You Can't Trust Me with a Choice, How Can You Trust Me with a Child?"; "Behind Every Successful Woman is Herself"; "What Part of 'NO' Don't You Understand?"; and "God Is Coming—and Is She Pissed."

From the Peace, Politics, Social Justice section I selected "The Earth Does Not Belong to Us, We Belong to the Earth"; "We All Live Downstream"; "Minds Are Like Parachutes, They Only Function When Open"; and that old standard, "Practice Random Kindness and Senseless Acts of Beauty." I was also so taken with the slogan "Nuke Gingrich" that I decided to order ten of them.

Last on my shopping list were buttons, which also went for $2 apiece. I figured that I already had the Animal Rights, Vegetarianism, Feminist, Racism, Environmental, Anti-Nuclear, Pre-Columbian, and Women's Issues angles pretty well covered with my T-shirts and bumper stickers, so I decided to take a pass on "Non-Violence Begins with the Fork" and the catchy "Women Constitute Half the World's

Population, Perform Nearly 2/3 of its Work Hours, Receive 1/10 of the World's Income, and Own Less than 1/100 of the World's Property." Instead, I opted for "Mute Newt"; "Think Globally, Act Locally"; "It Will be a Great Day When Our Schools Get All the Money They Need and the Air Force Has to Hold a Bake Sale to Buy a Bomber"; and "You Can't Hug Children with Nuclear Arms."

Since I have only one car, a legitimate question can be raised as to why I was stocking up on so many bumper stickers. Was I planning to change my bumper sticker slogan every day? Not at all. The truth was, earlier in my career I had done a number of stories about the collectibles market and had good reason to believe that some of these items might have great investment value a few years down the line. Twenty years ago, people would have laughed in your face if you had told them how much baseball cards and comic books would one day be worth. Today, they commanded Croesian fortunes. Something inside me suggested that the same could hold true for these plangent bumper stickers and buttons.

Particularly the one that read NUKE NEWT. By the time I embarked on my journey of spiritual rehabilitation, Newt Gingrich had already announced his retirement from the U.S. House of Representatives. Once he passed from the national scene, these buttons were going to be a lot less popular. The way I had things mapped out, I could buy about ten of these suckers, put them away for ten years, wait till they had become so rare that their value had skyrocketed, and then sell them on the open market. With the proceeds, I could help stop deforestation, strip mining, the rape of the rain forest, or perhaps even set up a philanthropic organization that would help belligerent people visualize world peace or live simply so that others might simply live. It would be my way of giving back something to a society that had given me so much. And wouldn't it piss off Newt!

When it actually came time to make my order, I found the No.H.A.R.M. website to be shockingly inefficient. For starters, you could only order six T-shirts or five bumper stickers and buttons at a time, but you could not order more than one of each item, because there was no box for "Quantity." Second, when I went back to the T-shirts section to check out the different colors and sizes that were available, my order form vanished from the screen and I had to fill it out all over again. Damnation. Third, the store did not take credit cards. *Hello? Can I speak to Mr. Luddite?* Fourth, there was no telephone number to call, because the entire website was electronic.

The experience put me in a bit of a bind. On the one hand, I was trying to be a good person, and understood that the people at the No.H.A.R.M. Store were trying to be good persons and to help me to be a good person too. Nevertheless, they were a smidgen incompetent. Yes, I was trying hard to respect the earth and all living creatures, which included the personnel at the No.H.A.R.M. Store, but I was also one of those people who honestly believed that if you wanted to make a nice omelet you had to break a few eggs. So I fired off a tersely worded E-mail to the No.H.A.R.M. folks telling them in no uncertain terms that their ordering system blew it right out the ass. And as soon as I was finished doing that, I went out to a Manhattan T-shirt store and had my own T-shirt printed up. It was bright red with all black letters and read

INCOMPETENCE IN THE SERVICE OF GOOD IS EVIL

Strongly worded? You betcha. But there was more than one way to subvert the dominant paradigm. And this was one of them.

Subconsciously, the joy derived from being able to write checks that made a moral and political statement impelled me to become more generous. Suddenly, I found myself writing breast-feeding checks to virtually every worthwhile cause in the land. I sent a check to the World Wildlife Fund and adopted a tiger. I sent a check to the Defenders of Wildlife and adopted a wolf. I sent a check to Steve Allen's Parents Television Council to prevent TV from leading our children down a moral sewer. And I sent a check to the Wilderness Society to protect our wetlands. Which was pretty amazing for me, because at the time I didn't even know what wetlands were. Finally, I ordered several pounds of shade-grown coffee. Once again, I did not actually know what shade-grown coffee was, but I figured it probably had something to do with the wetlands, and that Jackson Browne was somehow involved, so I felt that I was on pretty solid ground.

One thing I found was that the combination of writing all these checks while drinking shade-grown coffee was making me a much calmer person. A case in point: A few days after I sent my angry E-mail to the T-shirt folks up in Northhampton, I got a return E-mail from the proprietor apologizing for the unwieldy ordering system and also apologizing for not having some of the things I had ordered in stock. Since I had already written a check for $109, but he could only fulfill $69 of my order, he suggested that I send him a second check and tear up the first one. This was the kind of incompetence that got Che Guevara and the gang in trouble in the first place. Which is basically what I said in my next E-mail, remarking, "I just hope that when the revolution comes, you have better inventory control." Yet amazingly, I did not ream the guy out. Whereas the old me—say the person I had been four days earlier—would have been furious at such administrative ineptitude, the new Joe Queenan simply went with the flow. So determined was I to turn over a new leaf that I told the proprietor of the No.H.A.R.M. store to send me whatever merchandise he had and simply keep the rest of the money, because what he was doing was so noble and I was loaded anyway. If he had other T-shirts in my size, he should feel free to send them along; if not, he could make up the $40 by sending me bumper stickers and buttons and whatnot. This was the kind of informal commercial exchange that would already be routine in this society if Nixon hadn't gotten elected in 1968. It made me nostalgic for an earlier, more simple time when people didn't get all bent out of shape about money. If he didn't have the T-shirts I had ordered, then he didn't have the T-shirts I had ordered. It wasn't that big a deal.

While I waited for my goodness garb to arrive in the mail, I busied myself conducting a social audit of my personality, not unlike the corporate social audits I had seen in the back of Ben & Jerry's annual report. I figured it was important for me to get some solid data on what an appalling person I was, thereby sign-posting areas in which the greatest potential for personal growth existed. On a scale of one to ten, this is what I came up with:

Social Audit of Joe Queenan's Personality

Animal Testing. Briefly owned a hamster which died a natural death, thereby escaping the clutches of the perfume industry. But generally hated animals and did nothing to prevent their abuse by scientific researchers. **(1)**

Endangered Species. Once bought a howling toy wolf from the National Wildlife Federation. But the wolf was pathetic-looking and his children hated it, thereby precluding endangered-species consciousness-raising. **(1)**

The Environment. Absolutely nothing. **(0)**

Free Tibet. Attended several concerts in the early 1990s by the Tibetan Singing Bowl Ensemble, a New York group that used various implements to elicit ethereal sounds from ancient Tibetan cooking equipment. However, the founder of the group was Zero Mostel's nephew, a Jew from Passaic. **(2)**

Gay Rights. Had several gay friends and never used anti-gay material in his work or TV and radio appearances except once said on *Politically Incorrect* that the reason a gay cruise ship got turned away at a port in the Caribbean was because the island denizens could hear those Liza Minnelli records from hundreds of miles away and decided to act before it was too late. **(4)**

Manatees. Nothing. **(0)**

Minorities. Sent his kids to public school, which is more than you could say for most of his so-called liberal friends. But didn't go to public school himself because public schools in Philadelphia are death traps. **(4)**

Native Americans. Nothing. **(0)**

Nuclear Testing. Didn't seem to care one way or the other. **(0)**

The Poor. Had been one of them as a child, and didn't enjoy it. **(6)**

Rain Forest. Nothing. **(0)**

Redwoods. Hadn't even seen one. **(0)**

Snail Darter. Nothing. **(0)**

Whales. Knew that his wife was giving money to Greenpeace, and didn't object. Had read abridged version of *Moby Dick* in high school and thought the whale and Captain Ahab deserved each other. **(2)**

Women. Liked them, respected them, married one. **(6)**

Not a very pretty picture. Lots of work to be done.

The following Saturday morning, the T-shirts and bumper stickers arrived from Massachusetts. There was "It Takes a Whole Village." There was "Columbus Didn't Discover The New World...He Invaded It." There was "It Will Be a Great Day When Our Schools Get All the Money They Need and the Air Force Has to Hold a Bake Sale to Buy a Bomber." And there was "Practice Random Kindness and Senseless Acts of Beauty." I took it out of the package and slipped it on. I felt like a priest donning the cassock for the first time. It was time to get out there and start making a difference.

5 • Your Dad Must

Be the Nicest Man in

the Whole Wide World

When a spiritually undernourished person commits himself to a crash diet of moral protein and ethical riboflavin, there are two basic approaches he can take. The first is to follow the path of institutional virtue, as typified by organized religion, philanthropic foundations, and grassroots organizations such as Habitat for Humanity. In these environments, the infrastructure of righteousness is established by the visionaries, the guiding lights, the sacerdotes, while the participants, like worker bees, are asked to carry out the overarching program. This approach works well in stopping wars and spectacular miscarriages of injustice, or in spotlighting the hidden dangers posed to our children, poster and otherwise, by certain food additives, but it does not allow the participants much in the way of individual expression.

Having always been a bit of a maverick, a loner, a strong, silent type who dances to the beat of a different drummer, I preferred a more personal, creative approach to the philanthropic process. What I had in mind was the systematic implementation of a wide-ranging program of joyous philanthropy based on the cheerful messages emblazoned on my new collection of T-shirts. Primarily, I was thinking in terms of random acts of kindness and senseless acts of beauty. The advantage of performing random acts of kindness (henceforth referred to as RAKs) and senseless acts of beauty (henceforth referred to as SABs) was that it would spread an ineffable, subcutaneous tremor of bliss throughout the Republic, a palpable sense that good things could and would happen at entirely unexpected moments, and that ordinary people didn't have to wait for Jimmy Carter or Jackson Browne to show up in order for something really nice to happen to them.

Nothing better illustrates the evolution of the new Joe Queenan than my relationship with Sanjay Krishnaswamy. This is a name that may be unfamiliar to some readers, but it will not be for long. One day in the fall of 1998, when I was feeling in a particularly glum mood, as is often the case with morally calcified human beings, a strange letter arrived in the mail. The letter, mailed from Somerville, Massachusetts, had been addressed to my publisher and then, months later, forwarded to me.

The letter writer, Mr. Krishnaswamy, had recently read my book *Red Lobster, White Trash, and The Blue Lagoon*, and was highly impressed. He felt that the book "continued nicely in the great Mencken tradition of pop culture as zoology" and said that my "suffering and compassion" had earned his "deepest respect and admiration." He also said that he had enthusiastically recommended my book to "other elitist NPR-listening pricks" like him.

Still, heaping praise on me was not the reason he had written the letter. Instead, Mr. Krishnaswamy had noticed in reading *Red Lobster* that I was a big fan of Elvis Costello, and he was wondering if I might have in my possession an extremely rare recording Costello had made with the peerless jazz guitarist Bill Frisell. The album was entitled *Deep*

Dead Blue. Mr. Krishnaswamy informed me that he had been looking for the album for years, but had never laid eyes on it. He also assured me that the album was not a crass bootleg, but "a limited release in Europe only." Since I was "a published writer with contacts and resources" he so conspicuously lacked, he thought that I might either own the album or knew where to get it. If so, he would be overjoyed if I would make him a copy, and ship it up to Somerville. He said he would "happily pick up any shipping charges."

Upon finishing this letter, I flew into a rage. I had always imagined that when I finally wrote a book that landed on best-seller lists, I would be lauded by the *cognoscenti*, feted by the *literati*, and cosseted by the gentry, and that from this point onward life would be nothing but Panama hats, linen suits, and $50 cigars. But no, it was the same crap as usual, with complete strangers writing to ask if I could make a copy of an Elvis Costello CD I didn't even own and then hustle down to the post office to mail it to them. Mind you—without even sending me a blank tape.

The whole issue of "favors" had long been a touchy subject with me. Eight months earlier I'd made a short film for Britain's artsy Channel 4 entitled *So You Wanna Be a Gangster*, which dealt with a successful writer living in Tarrytown, New York, who gets so fed up with his neighbors asking if he can get their kids jobs on *Letterman* or read their screenplays or find an agent for their novels or persuade Don Imus to emcee their charity bake-athons that he joins the Mafia and learns how to break people's legs. Now, a complete stranger living several hundred miles away who wasn't even that big a fan of my work was asking me to make a copy of a record by Elvis Costello, whose work he wasn't that big a fan of, either, and send it to him. As if I had nothing better to do with my time. Jesus, I wished I had become a mobster.

Needless to say, I ripped up the letter and threw it into the trash. But later that night, I retrieved it because I wanted to include it in my ever-expanding file of Fiendishly Annoying Letters from So-called Fans, which I intended to one day fashion into an op-ed piece about the trials and tribulations of being a freelance writer. Then I forgot about it.

Fast-forward to the winter of 1999. One day, as I am sifting through my old mail I come upon Mr. Krishnaswamy's letter once again. As when I first received it, I am amazed at the naivete of someone who would actually believe that I had nothing better to do with my time than to send complete strangers audiotaped copies of obscure compact discs that I didn't even own. Like, *the nerve.*

But then I got to thinking about it. If I was really serious about practicing RAKs and SABs, wasn't this a good place to begin? Here was a person who had reached out to me, not really expecting to get anything in return. (If he'd expected me to respond, he would have sent a blank tape.) So wouldn't it be nice if I reciprocated the gesture by at least answering my fan mail for the first time in my life? No, better still, wouldn't it be nice if I did a bit of legwork for a fellow who seemed to be a very nice young man?

The next afternoon, I began looking for the mysterious CD. Well, believe you me, I searched high and I searched low. I visited big midtown stores like Virgin and Tower Records and I haunted musty old used-CD stores located far from the maddening crowd in deeply ironic neighborhoods. My quest was not crowned with success. In the first nineteen stores I checked, no one had ever heard of the CD. At a couple of stores, I was told I must be thinking of *Almost Blue,* the flawed but essentially wonderful country & western record Costello had made in Nashville in the early eighties.

"I think Lefty Frizzell might be on that record," the owner of one shop told me. Lefty Frizzell is, of course, the C &W legend who wrote such songs as "That's the Way Love Goes." But I was sure that Frizzell had never made a record with Elvis Costello, and anyway, none of this had anything to do with Bill Frisell, a jazz guitarist.

"First time I heard of it," said a salesman at Venus Sounds on St. Mark's Place, in the heart of Manhattan's studiously grubby East Village.

"I think it might be an EP or a bootleg or an import or an imported bootleg EP," I explained, trying to stir some interest.

"First time I ever heard of it," the man replied.

"It could be a limited edition or a novelty item," I volunteered.

"First time I ever heard of it."

This went on for quite a few weeks. Periodically, I would check eBay, the online auction site, to see if the record had ever been sold over the Internet, but it never surfaced. One day my editor mentioned that she knew how to get into touch with Mr. Costello, whom I had in fact met on the rooftop of the Bel Age Hotel in Los Angeles in 1994 when he was mixing *Brutal Youth* and I was the fifth-to-last guest on the doomed *Chevy Chase Show.* Mr. Costello was just about the most charming, interesting person I had ever met in the entertainment industry, delighting me with stories about Nick Lowe and unexpected observations about Franz Liszt, so it was not entirely out of the question that I might write him and ask

1) Did you ever make a CD with Bill Frisell?

2) If so, do you have a copy I could borrow?

3) If not, do you think it's a record you might consider making, as there seem to be a lot of fans out there who not only would buy it, but already believe that it exists?

Ultimately, I decided that I would not importune Mr. Costello until all other options had been exhausted, for the simple reason that he would get my letter and think: "Gee, I always figured that once I got to make a critically acclaimed record with the legendary Burt Bacharach, it would be nothing but Panama hats, linen suits, and $50 cigars, but here I am getting a letter from some dip-shit journalist who claims to have met me five years ago when he was doing *The Chevy Chase Show* asking if I could make a record with Bill Frisell. *As if I had nothing better to do with my time!*"

Luckily, this intrusion was not necessary. One afternoon when I was in the East Village, I stopped by my favorite record store, St. Mark's Sounds. While thumbing through the stacks, it occurred to me that the last two times I had visited the store the salesman had been too busy to answer my questions. Today the store was empty. So now seemed like a good time to ask if he had ever heard of *Deep Dead Blue.*

"I'll see if I still have a copy of that," the always helpful young man said, dashing off to the back room. *Oh, my God,* I thought. *It actually exists.* Someone has actually seen it. I was *this* close to hitting pay dirt.

A few seconds later, the man returned, shaking his head.

"I don't have any more," he said.

"But it exists?" I said. "You've actually seen it?"

"Oh yeah, it exists," he replied. "It's an EP."

He then recommended several places I might check out. I immediately did so. I went to a nearby store specializing in musical rarities. They had never heard of it. I dropped by the redoubtable Bleecker Bob's. They had never heard of it. I visited seven other stores in the East Village. No one had ever seen or heard of it. So now I was starting to think that the man at St. Mark's Sounds had been mistaken, that the record he was thinking of was in fact *Almost Blue*. Because even though he had seen it, and claimed to have stocked it, and said that he had sold it, he did not say that he had actually *heard* it. So it might all be an illusion.

Then a second merchant confirmed its existence.

"Every once in a while we get a copy of it," said the proprietor of Norman Sound & Vision, a very fine CD store on the Bowery, just a few steps from St. Mark's Place. "It's excellent. It exists. It definitely exists."

Well, that certainly bucked me up. But the best was yet to come. Continuing my quest for the Holy Grail, I drifted past the legendary Bottom Line, where Dave Davies, lead guitarist of the legendary Kinks and brother of Ray Davies, was playing that rainy evening. The show was slated to start at 7:30, but there was an opening act and opening acts are always horrendous, so Dave probably wouldn't come on till about 8:45 and it was only 6:45, so that gave me about two hours to kill walking around looking for *Deep Dead Blue*. (At this point in my odyssey, I could only muster the moral fiber to do one good thing at a time, so it never even occurred to me that going to see the dreadful opening act was precisely the kind of selfless gesture that Saint Francis of Assisi and Gandhi were celebrated for. Later, as the floodgates of virtue began to sluice through my nervous system, I came to realize that precisely because they *are* pathetic, opening acts are fitting subjects for our charity and affection. So I went to see a lot of them, sitting through every number in their dreary sets. I am not suggesting for an instant that opening acts are not appalling, or that I ever stopped thinking that they were appalling, just as Father Damien of Molokai never lost sight of the fact that leprosy was gross. It was, in fact, the fact that they were appalling, and that I knew that they were appalling, that made my going to see them such a hierophantic gesture of translucent altruism. But I digress.)

In any case, while I was wandering through the streets of Soho in the rain, it started to rain harder. Seeking shelter from the storm, I ducked into a used-CD store on West Bleecker Street. At the front of the store was a copious selection of Elvis Costello CDs. As I had done so many other times over the course of the past few months, I rifled through the CDs. Only this time, to my utter disbelief, there it was: a seven-song EP made in Germany in 1995 featuring the Costello classic "Love Field," plus such odd selections as "Gigi." Enthralled, I raced to the cashier, plunked down my $16.95, and nipped out into the rain, rejoicing.

Although Dave Davies's fettle could not have been finer that evening, the real reason my heart would not stop racing was because I had finally tracked down the elusive Elvis Costello–Bill Frisell collaboration, and was now in a position to consummate my first random act of senseless beauty. After the concert, I rushed home and cued up the CD. A solid effort it was! Frisell's lean, mysterious guitar work had never been better, and Costello's harrowing vocals were imbued with the truculent vulnerability for which he is almost intergalactically famous. Mr. Krishnaswamy would soon find that his epistolatory endeavors were to pay off in spades.

Now although I am the kind of person who is more than willing to spend month after month looking for a rare, possibly nonexistent compact disc for a person I have never met, I am not the kind of person who will, under any circumstances, sit down and make tape recordings (too annoying, too proletarian, too much drudgery). That's why I decided the next morning to simply mail the CD to Mr. Krishnaswamy with a nice little note and wish him godspeed. But then I had a better idea. Spending weeks diligently beating the bushes for an obscure Elvis Costello–Bill Frisell CD that would then be shipped off to a complete stranger certainly qualified as a RAK. But it was not nearly as randomly beautiful and senselessly kind as going that extra mile. The one thing I had learned from my study of the great philanthropists from Jesus

Christ to Harry Belafonte was that virtue was most effective when it was obstreperous and plangent. What Christ, Saint Francis and, yes, even Jackson Browne aimed at when they performed good deeds was to augment the mythology of virtue. The bigger the effort, the more spectacular the deed, the farther the legend of one's largess would spread through the hinterland. In short, it wouldn't suffice for me to send *Deep Dead Blue* to Mr. Krishnaswamy. I had to personally deliver it.

Somerville, Massachusetts, a tumble-down suburb that abuts stately Cambridge, is roughly a four-hour drive from Tarrytown, New York, but, as luck would have it, the kids were off from school the next week and the whole family has always loved Boston, so off we trundled to venerable Beantown. Pretending to be a delivery man, I phoned Mr. Krishnaswamy the night before I left Tarrytown to make sure that he would be in the next day. He said he would be there until two in the afternoon, but did not bother to ask what was being delivered.

The trip to Boston was uneventful. We arrived in Somerville at about 1:15, but got inaccurate directions from the typically hapless locals, and did not arrive at Mr. Krishnaswamy's apartment until ten past two. Luckily, he was still there. When my daughter and I knocked on his front door, out popped a tall, spindly Indian-American with a mammoth ponytail. Usually I do not like men in ponytails, especially when they are middle-aged, or waiters, or middle-aged waiters, but Sanjay radiated an obvious warmth and charm, and I had no reason to believe he was a waiter, so I decided to ignore my prejudice. Besides, ponytails are part of that whole subcontinental thing, so what the heck?

Although my photograph had appeared on the cover of the book that had piqued Sanjay's interest in the first place, it was clear that he did not immediately recognize me and certainly did not recognize my daughter. Not one to stand on ceremony, I thrust the compact disc into his hand, saying, "I understand that you've been looking for this for some time. Well, here it is."

When he saw the cover of the CD, Sanjay gasped.

"I've been looking for this for years!" he exclaimed. "But...how..."

"I'm Joe Queenan," I explained.

"You *are* Joe Queenan!" he agreed. "I wrote you that letter asking if you had this record…"

"Yes," I said. "And I didn't have it. But I went out and found it. And here it is."

Sanjay was still too flabbergasted to speak.

"Can we come in?" I inquired.

Of course we could. My daughter and I entered a small room filled with musical instruments, books, an impressive collection of compact discs, and several exotic birds. There was a toucan, an African gray, a lovebird, and some parakeets or budgerigars (I do not know the difference between the two species). Sanjay, a vivacious, excitable sort, immediately began demonstrating the birds' remarkable skills to my enthralled daughter. Meanwhile, my wife and son joined us. Sanjay, still marveling over this unexpected visit, offered us coffee and tea, then escorted the children into the backyard to try out his three-story tree house, which provided an excellent view of the Charles River. Meanwhile, he asked how I'd come to find the compact disc. I explained that I had spent a small eternity looking for it, and had finally tracked it down, and then had decided to personally deliver it.

"Why?" he asked.

"Because that's the kind of person I am," I explained. "Besides, I didn't have anything better to do with my time. And because I believe in letting a thousand flowers bloom."

Hearing this, Sanjay stared at the CD, flicked on his head-beam smile, and turned to my daughter.

"Your dad must be the nicest man in the whole wide world," he informed her.

I'd been waiting my entire life to hear these words.

Virtuous people will tell you that the love you give is equal to the love you make, and this was more or less the case here. Although the compact disc cost me $16.95, plus countless lost hours of hunting for it, and the trip to Boston set me back $372 for the hotel, $250 for meals, $30 for gas, and $109 for sundries, not to mention three days of lost work, which I clock at a minimum one thousand bucks a day, this SAB paid off in more ways than one. Sure, I derived the immense psychic rewards of not only being called, but actually believing, that I was the best dad in the whole wide world, a kudo all patresfamilias covet. But there were also tangible benefits to the trip. For one, I got to see the Mary Cassatt show that was visiting the Boston Museum of Fine Arts. And the kids got to climb up Bunker Hill monument and walk the Freedom Trail and visit Paul Revere's house.

But that was only the tip of the Good Samaritanial iceberg. Sanjay, it developed, was an astrophysicist with a special interest in fiber-optics who had attended Harvard University. So my daughter, a math whiz, and our host got on like a house on fire. That afternoon, Sanjay gave us an extensive tour of the university, spotlighting all the nooks and crannies, pointing out amusing architectural anomalies, charming us with Cambridgean lore. He also took us on a trip through the overwrought commercial district of the town.

Before that visit, my daughter had been thinking about applying to Harvard, but after she saw what a tourist trap Cambridge was she decided it was not for her. Since a four-year program at Harvard, should she be accepted, would run $160,000, my visit had literally saved me tens of thousands of dollars. All of which seemed to be a vivid confirmation of the Butterfly Theory, which states that if a person in Beijing releases a butterfly, the ripple effect can cause an earthquake in Manhattan. Or, in this case, if one person in Somerville, Massachusetts, writes a letter to someone in Tarrytown, New York, asking if he can make a copy of an Elvis Costello–Bill Frisell CD, the second person's daughter may end up going to SUNY-Binghamton or Holy Cross, instead of Harvard (preferably with some financial aid), thereby saving him a bundle.

I should point out that before Sanjay and I parted company, I gave him a blank Maxell tape and told him to record the CD for himself and then give me back the original, as his letter had specifically requested a tape and not the CD. I did this because I had taken a shine to the quirky CD and didn't feel like spending another small eternity looking for a copy. And because no matter how much I liked the CD, I was serious when I said that *I don't make tapes.*

Just before I left Boston, Sanjay told me that he had heard that Warner Brothers was planning to rerelease the CD, making it widely available in stores all around the country. When I got back to New York, a good friend said that the CD had recently been auctioned for $3 on the Internet. I also found a second copy for just $10 one afternoon when I wasn't even looking for it. None of this invalidated the overall moral value of the good deed I had done. If anything, it heightened it, because now it was not only a *truly random* act of kindness, but a *completely senseless* act of beauty.

It was not very long before a second opportunity to practice a RAK presented itself. One day I received a call from the *Imus in the Morning* show, inviting me to participate in the first annual Don Imus's American Book Awards, which would be held in front of a live audience at the 92nd Street Y in New York City. One year earlier Imus had launched his own awards program because he was upset at the National Book Awards people for failing to honor Sam Tanenhaus, author of *Whittaker Chambers*, instead giving the top nonfiction prize to one of the usual suspects. Imus was offering three prizes of $50,000 apiece and one $100,000 grand prize. Two of the prize-winning books, including the $100,000 one, would be selected by the host himself. The other two would be decided by shoppers visiting Barnes & Noble bookstores or voting online at barnesandnoble.com. The books had been selected by a panel of five judges handpicked by Esther Newberg, Imus's literary agent, and quite a usual suspect in her own right.

I was more than happy to appear on the program because it gave me a chance to make fun of crackpots like Lani Guinier and the over-praised Papa Hemingway clone Cormac McCarthy. I arrived around seven in the morning, went on around 7:30, and had a rip-roaring good time upbraiding Imus for his failure to give me the award. I poked fun at the selection process, noting that several of the books had been huge stiffs, and suggested that Imus was doing the editors of these under-performing mutts a favor by breathing some life into their corpses. I also pointed out that Sam Tanenhaus, my neighbor in Tarrytown, might well be honored to have set in motion the apparatus that led to the establishment of the first annual Don Imus's American Book Awards, but he himself wasn't getting a goddamned nickel out of the deal, because Imus was not retroactively honoring his book with a substantial cash emolument. Which sounded to me like an even bigger ream job than getting screwed out of the National Book Award the year before.

Things were going along swimmingly until the time came to announce the winner of the $50,000 prize for fiction. The finalists were McCarthy, the talented Richard Price, and four women whose names I did not recognize: Susan Dodd, Martha Cooley, Ruth Ozeki, and Edwidge Danticat. Cooley had written a novel called *The Archivist*, which had something to do with T. S. Eliot; Ozeki had written a book called *My Year of Meats*, which was a cross-cultural look at the feminist beef industry or something; Danticat had written *The Farming of Bones*, which dealt with the 1937 massacre of 20,000 Haitian immigrants in the Dominican Republic; and Dodd had written a novel that was wistful. None of them sounded like Don Imus kind of books. And they certainly didn't sound like Bernard McGuirk kind of books.

Eventually, Imus announced the winner. It was Edwidge Danticat, the woman from Haiti. A huge check for $50,000 was produced with her name written on it. A few wisecracks were exchanged, then we went back to our casual banter. But suddenly word came from the back room that the wrong prize winner had been announced. Apparently, the folks backstage had run the numbers incorrectly, because the real winner was not Edwidge Danticat but Ruth Ozeki, author of *My Year of Meats*. So Don announced that Danticat was not getting the fifty grand after all, that it was going to the legitimate winner, Ozeki, who had been shafted because of a procedural error.

Frankly, I was aghast. Lambasting Imus's "first-class operation," I told him that the right thing to do would be to split the prize, because Danticat would be crushed to learn that she had won $50,000 and then have the prize ripped from her grasp. "She's already bought the Gran Torino," I explained, impassioned. But Imus and his sidekick Charles McCord ignored me. They insisted that the incorrect announcement was the result of a clerical error, that it was not their fault, that there was nothing to be done.

I, on the other hand, could clearly delineate the poignant subterranean moral issues here. While it was true that Danticat had not actually won the prize in question, the mere fact that she had been told that she had won, and then been informed that it was all a mistake, was like surviving the firing squad and then being told it was time for the hanging. No one had any way of knowing how Danticat would react to this cruel turn of events. If she were at all emotionally fragile, it could devastate her for life. Trust me, reader: I knew whereof I spoke. I was still totally devastated that some nincompoop like Lani Guinier might be pocketing fifty large while I was going home with the Big Nada.

When it became clear that Imus was not going to do anything to rectify this horrible snafu, I stepped into the breach, announcing right then and there that I was setting up my own Annual Book Awards which would dispense substantial cash prizes to people who had been screwed out of their Don Imus American Book Awards because of clerical errors by his inept staffers. Specifically, I vowed to pay Danticat $1,000 for getting cheated out of her prize. Then I told a few more jokes, insulted a few more people, and left.

Was I serious about writing Danticat a check for $1,000? Yes, I was. Why? Because it was precisely the kind of "noisy philanthropy" that was practiced by Paul Newman, Bette Midler, Sting, Susan Sarandon, and many other exquisite human beings of peerless ethical pedigree. It was the kind of noble gesture that would reverberate throughout American society, perhaps becoming a staple of American folklore, taking its place alongside Johnny Appleseed's tin hat, George Washington's tiny axe, and Davy Crockett's coonskin cap. Because it was such a poignant RAK, and one that I could talk about on the radio the next time I was a guest on *Imus,* it would send a message to the people of America that if a cold-hearted bastard like Joe Queenan could give away $1,000 of his hard-earned money to the Haitian author of a novel he had no intention of ever reading, then anyone could mend their ways and be all that they could be.

Obviously, not everybody took me at my word. One week after my appearance at the awards ceremony, I received a perplexing phone call from a crusading journalist named Philip Nobile. For some time, Nobile had been obsessed with portraying Imus and his crew as hopeless racists. At the awards ceremony, he had actually tried to distribute a leaflet saying IMUS = RACISM & HOMOPHOBIA and had been thrown out of the 92nd Street Y for doing so. Nobile now demanded to know if I had yet made good on my promise to write a check for $1,000 to Danticat. It was obvious from his tone that he thought I had been joking, that I had no real plans to honor my commitment. Clearly he thought I was a run-of-the-mill poser, a charlatan, a fake.

This was not true. My dismay at the way the awards ceremony had been handled was genuine, and I had every intention of affixing my John Hancock to that check. But I must say, I didn't care much for Nobile's inquisitorial style. Which put me in a bit of a predicament. If I immediately wrote the check it might seem that I was only doing so because Nobile had backed me into a corner, called my bluff, forced me over a barrel, or all of the above. But if I didn't write the check, it would look like I was a phony.

That wasn't all. After Nobile and I had finished discussing my awards program, he grilled me on my thoughts about Don Imus, putative racist. This conversation went nowhere. Nobile obviously thought I was refusing to say anything negative about Imus because I was fearful that by doing so I would forfeit any chance of ever again being on his show. Little did he know that I was already working on a book about people who practiced ostentatious virtue of Imusian ilk, and was obviously not worried one way or the other about what Imus thought of my work. More to the point, I resented Nobile's badgering the witness. When he realized that he could not get me to go along with his verdict on Imus, we hit an unhappy impasse. Eventually, I told him that we had talked long enough, and slammed down the phone.

After I slammed down the phone, I felt a pang of remorse. It was quite evident that Nobile was not the world's most gifted journalist, and was a reporter whose career had probably been handicapped by a prosecutorial interviewing style that probably resulted in many premature hang-ups. And yes, I would be lying if I did not admit that I found him to be a bit of a jerk. But just because he was a jerk didn't mean that I had the right to slam down the phone on him. When I thought back on the great men and women of the past that I had been attempting to emulate, I had to admit that Saint Francis of Assisi would not have slammed down the phone on Nobile, nor would have Gandhi or Buddha or Johnny Appleseed or Saint Claire or Ben Cohen and Jerry Greenfield or Jesus, or, for that matter, Jackson Browne. So I decided to find Nobile's number and apologize to him for being rude. I would do this just as soon as I could get hold of that unfortunate Haitian novelist.

Alas, contriteness is not part of my emotional makeup. Because of what Cromwell did to my Irish forebears, because of the potato famine, and because I had grown up on the mean streets of Philadelphia, I simply could not bring myself to make that call. It turned out not to be necessary. A short time later, I got a second call from Nobile requesting an update on my award to Ms. Danticat. I patiently explained to him that my Awards Foundation did not like being browbeaten, because it would make us look callow and malleable. Detecting an emotional guffaw at the other end of the line, I asked Nobile point-blank if he thought I was not going to write the check. He said he didn't know if I was the kind of person who welshed on my promises, that perhaps I was the kind of person who had to pay to send his kids to private school, and might be strapped for cash. Whereupon I gave Nobile a very severe tongue-lashing. I told him that he did not know me, did not know my values, and obviously did not know that my kids went to public school and not to some epicene institution replete with headmasters and fowlers. After I had finished chastising him, I said that the only way Ms. Danticat was ever going to get her money was if he promised to stop calling me. This he said he would do. At the end of our rather testy exchange, Nobile thanked me for taking his call, noting that he did not get much repeat business from people he interviewed. This rendered my contemplated apology superfluous, as Nobile had as much as said that anyone who would take his calls was already practicing charity on a rather spectacular level.

Shortly thereafter, I wrote the check to Ms. Danticat. I waited awhile to do it only because I had not yet received my Message!Checks with the picture of the breast-feeding mother and infant emblazoned on them. To my great irritation, it took several weeks to get my hands on the checks. That's because when they arrived in the mail, my wife opened the package, thought it was a practical joke—since it was so unlike me to take a principled stand on anything—and threw them into the junk mail pile. When I accidentally stumbled upon them, I immediately wrote the check to the Haitian novelist, then found out the name of her agent, to whom I sent a note asking her to pass along the following letter:

>Dear Ms. Danticat,
>
>As you know, I was a guest on *Imus in the Morning* the day you got shanghaied out of that $50,000 prize for best fiction book. When my strenuous efforts to persuade Don to split the prize with the eventual winner were unsuccessful, I announced that I was going to set up my own Annual Awards that would seek to make up for any arithmetical or procedural errors committed by Don Imus's staff. Specifically, I said that I was going to write you a check for $1,000 to help ease the sting of this most egregious ream job. Though your agent assures me that you took the incident in stride, adopting a *c'est la vie* attitude toward the lost cash, I think you have every right to be hopping mad. May I add that while I admire your composure, aplomb, *sang-froid,* and ability to roll with the punches, rest assured that if anybody ever tried screwing me out of fifty large, I'd be out the door shopping for a new tire iron and a couple dozen hand grenades faster than you could say, "It doesn't get any better than this."
>
>Enclosed please find a check for $1,000, the first annual award issued by the Joe Queenan Imus American Book Awards Rectification Foundation. We certainly hope that we don't have to write many of these checks in the years to come, but based on the level of professionalism witnessed in 1999, I suspect that the Foundation could be very active with the pocketbook for decades in the future. Spend the money as you wish and be of good cheer, whatever that might entail.
>
>One final note: Shortly after the Imus Awards imbroglio, I was contacted by marauding journalist Philip Nobile, who demanded to know when and if I was going to make good on

my promise to send you the thousand bucks. I told him that I didn't like being pressured and would send the money when I was good and ready. I don't think he believed me, because he called back just recently and asked the exact same question, even intimating that I might be the kind of person who welshes on my commitments. Interestingly, Nobile was upset with me because I refused to attack Don Imus's supposedly "racist" material, but Nobile himself used the term "welsh," which is offensive to every man, woman, and child in the great nation of Wales. In other words, the foot knoweth neither the shoe nor the mouth that it fitteth.

Anyway, when I couldn't get this ding-dong off the phone, I repeated my comment that neither I nor my foundation would allow itself to be browbeaten by roving knuckleheads of his ilk. In other words I do not want you to think that I am sending you this check because of pressure from that irksome peckerwood, as I am incredibly cheap and would rather die than give away my hard-earned money. So if he calls you up and demands some kind of commission, just tell him to take a hike.

Best wishes with all your projects.

Joe Queenan

By this point, I had shelled out approximately $1,900 on RAKs and SABs. How did I feel? I can truthfully say that nothing I had ever done in my life ever gave me as much pleasure, or reaffirmed my worth as a human being, as much as these two selfless gestures of randomly senseless beauty. If I were the CEO of my own socially conscious Vermont-based premium ice-cream company, I immediately would have concocted a flavor called Philly Joe Crunch, and recounted my philanthropic exploits on the side of each container, thus encouraging other Americans to engage in similar displays of munificent bonhomie. I did not own such an enterprise, so this chapter will have to suffice as a personal testament to my virtue. Let me make clear that I did what I did not because I am a better person than my readers, though this may be the case, but because I truly and sincerely believe that the practice of ostentatious philanthropy is the only way we can teach our children well to do the right thing. In saying this, I am not blowing my own horn. I am not lighting a candle in the wind rather than cursing the darkness. I am merely shouting from the mountaintops that RAKs worked for me, and they may well work for you. So get out the checkbooks. Preferably hemp-based. And start writing.

6 . Family Values

One question that needs to be answered is how my family reacted to my unexpected quest for spiritual and moral rehabilitation. Because I had dragged my daughter to see Liza Minnelli in *Victor/Victoria* and had forced my son to spend an afternoon in the company of stout yeomen and Merovingian cutpurses at Ye Olde Renaissance Faire when I was writing my last book, my children were initially quite apprehensive about where this new enterprise might lead. Basically, they were willing to go along with my program as long as it did not involve immense personal humiliation, like being forced to attend a Holly Near concert or wear Support the Tree Lady T-shirts.

But they were not terribly enthusiastic about the enterprise, and they were not always that cooperative.

A case in point. One day I spied a headline in the *New York Post* reading, ALEC SEEKS OUT TOOTH ABOUT RADIATION. The article explained that Alec Baldwin, one of the most persistently virtuous people on the planet today, was "asking parents in New York and New Jersey to donate their children's baby teeth to science rather than the tooth fairy." According to the story, an organization called the Radiation and Public Health Project was hoping to collect one thousand baby teeth by December 31, 1999, in order to determine if nuclear reactors in the greater New York metropolitan area were transmitting radiation to small children. To achieve this, the organization was actively seeking one or two baby teeth from children aged five through twelve.

It just so happened that my son Gordon had recently turned twelve and had a baby tooth that was coming loose. One night at dinner I asked if he would pass along the tooth when it finally did fall out of his mouth.

"How much will you give me?" he demanded.

"Why should I give you anything?" I fired back.

"Because I always get money from the tooth fairy."

"Gord, you don't believe in the tooth fairy."

"Yes, I do," he replied.

"No, you don't," I insisted. "You stopped believing in the Tooth Fairy the same time you stopped believing in the Easter Bunny."

"If I give you the tooth, I expect to be compensated," he said, ignoring my arguments.

Impressed though I was by his use of the word "compensated," this attitude left me crestfallen. Obviously, the money was not the problem. But it crushed me that my own flesh and blood didn't see the larger issue here, the fact that we—Gord, Alec, mankind, Kim—all lived downstream, we were all in this together, and we needed to pool our resources for the benefit of humanity. This was the sort of thing I would have expected him to learn at school or from watching *Captain Planet*. Obviously, I was wrong.

Eventually, the tooth fell out and Gord forked it over. I in turn gave him five bucks for his efforts. Gord then volunteered to donate any other teeth that might fall out, but I had a sneaking suspicion that the little mercenary could no longer be trusted, that he would deliberately get into fights with some of his chums, knock out their teeth, and then try to pass them off as his own just to pocket a fast sawbuck. For the first time in my life, I was confronted with the genetic fallout from my own deep cynicism and shocking lack of philanthropy. It was true that the apple fell not far from the tree. And just like the young me, Gord had the makings of one very bad apple.

The next day, I sent a letter to the upstanding organization. It read:

> Radiation and Public Health Project
> P.O. Box 60
> Unionville, NY 10988
>
> Dear Sir or Ms.,
> I read about your project a few weeks ago in the *New York Post*, of all places. (Disgusting right-wing rag!) I have long been interested in any project supported by Alec Baldwin; a few years ago, when he became involved in that effort to put an end to international parrot smuggling, I even bought my kids a "talking" parrot and recorded environmentally sensitive messages on it. (As you can well imagine, the little rapscallions quickly substituted swear words, but never mind.) In any case, I am sending you a tooth that has just fallen out of my 12-year-old son's mouth. (I actually had to pay the little bastard $5, as he was holding out for a better offer from the tooth fairy. Kids!!!!) The tooth is not in such great shape, as it has been lying around my office for a few days, but it is my understanding that nuclear radiation lasts for millions of years, so I suspect you can still make some use of it. Please let me know anything else I can do to help your cause—I might even consider knocking a couple of teeth out of the little kid's mouth if it would help advance the cause of humanity. (Only joking!!!)
> Please let me know how your study turns out. We only

have one planet, and I appreciate your efforts to make it a safe one.

If you see Alec, give him a high five for me.

Best Wishes,

Joe Queenan

Almost immediately, I received a letter from the Radiation and Health Project informing me that "Alec will be thrilled" to get the tooth, and then asking me to fill out a form supplying all the relevant data about the tooth's history. I asked my son to fill out the form, but he was pissed off at me for rejecting his offer of additional nuclear dentition, so I had to fill it out myself.

On other issues, my family was even less accommodating. When my wife, who donates money to Amnesty International, Greenpeace, Hale House, the Red Cross, the Children's Aid Society, Planned Parenthood, Save the Children, MADD, Helen Keller International, and a number of local causes, who is a board member of the Tarrytown Foundation for the Public Schools, who is a member of the Tarrytown Garden Club, and who is president of the Tarrytown Neighborhood House, a center that looks out for senior citizens, none of which she is compensated for, was informed that I had ordered a bevy of bumper stickers from the No.I.I.A.R.M. Store, and that she could have the pick of the litter, she exploded with uncharacteristic fury.

"No bumper stickers!" she snapped. "None of that Practice Random Kindness stuff on my car. Put them on your bike."

Here I was in a real bind. I had sent away for all these bumper stickers, figuring to change our family slogan once a month, and now my wife was telling me that she wouldn't let me put any of the bumper stickers on the car.

"But I ordered *It Takes a Whole Village* and *Columbus Didn't Discover The New World…He Invaded It* and *It Will Be a Great Day When Our Schools Get All the Money They Need and the Air Force Has to Hold a Bake Sale to Buy a Bomber….*," I protested.

"No bumper stickers!" she declared. And that was the end of that.

I was disappointed that my wife had taken such a hard line on this issue. Obviously, she felt that this, like so many of my other activities, was a stunt designed to generate comic material but leave our household utterly disgraced. Moreover, I think she resented my impetuous *anschluss* into the philanthropic milieu that had always been her exclusive domain. My wife had always been a good and caring person, while I had always been a bastard. If I started practicing RAKs, it would make her RAKs look less impressive, because my RAKs were better bankrolled, because I was the one who bought Microsoft at 29.

There were many other areas in which my newfound virtue dramatically affected our lives. From the time I started buying records in 1963 until the spring of 1999, I had accumulated 495 LPs, 725 CDs, and 125 cassettes, of which 365 were classical, 148 were jazz, about 35 were country and western, 42 were unclassifiable (*Chieftains VIII, John Fahey's Greatest Hits, The Phantastic Phillies*), and the remaining 755 were rock, rhythm and blues, soul, or folk. One day, I set myself the task of determining how many of my records had been made by artists who could truly be described as people trying to make the world better through their art. The results were shocking. I owned one Peter Gabriel CD, one U2 CD, one Pete Seeger/Arlo Guthrie LP, Sting's *Greatest Hits* CD, two Billy Bragg cult classics, and a handful of records by Springsteen and REM. All told, I counted 14 socially conscious CDs, just 7 if you eliminated REM, and 32 socially conscious LPS, 8 if you threw out REM, Springsteen, the Police, and early Dylan (I was really stretching here). Dragging out old LPs I never listened to anymore, I did unearth a pair of Country Joe McDonald LPs and a record Willie Nelson (Farm Aid) made a long time ago with Leon Russell. But that was about it.

Even when I generously expanded my definition of socially conscious performers to include Dire Straits and Eric Clapton, because they had performed at Live Aid, and k. d. lang, because she was k. d. lang, I could find only 32 CDs and 47 records in my mammoth collection that fit the socially conscious criteria I had delineated. (For whatever the reason, I had never purchased any *tapes* by people who were trying to improve the human condition.) It was all surly icons like the Stones, Bowie, or Prince, cult figures like Richard Thompson, or self-absorbed oddballs like Warren Zevon, Iggy Pop, and Graham Parker. Nothing more succinctly described the type of person I was than that I owned 6

George Harrison LPs, not to mention both Travelin' Wilburys CDs, but had never bought *The Concert for Bangladesh*. Everybody in my generation owned *The Concert for Bangladesh*.

Once I had made these calculations, I set aside a special side on my shelf for these anointed artists. Henceforth, I decided, I would banish the bulk of my record collection to the beet cellar, and make sure that my CD player, my tape deck, and my turntable never featured anything that was not in some way associated with the amelioration of the human, mammalian, avian, floral, faunal, or fungal condition. From that point on, the only things we heard in my house were Pete Seeger's songs about cleaning up the Hudson River or Country Joe McDonald's rendition of Woody Guthrie's "Roll on, Columbia, Roll on." My kids started spending a lot of time in their rooms.

Another reason my kids started spending a lot of time in their rooms was my new policy regarding family-room entertainment. Here, I am basically talking about films. One evening it occurred to me that a truly caring RAK would be to support artists who had espoused important causes by renting their worst movies. Not the worst in the artistic sense, but in the sense that they had tanked at the box office, though the two were usually one and the same. The idea here was that no matter how bad the movies were, my renting them and encouraging friends to rent them would help the crusading artists' careers, and leave them with more time and money to save the rain forest or the spirit bear or the whales.

So each and every day, I would rent at least one dreadful film by Susan Sarandon, Robin Williams, Alec Baldwin, Nicole Kidman, Kim Basinger, Billy Crystal, Whoopi Goldberg, or another artist of this genre. Although I derived immense psychological satisfaction from this generous act of cultural self-crucifixion, I cannot say that it was an easy task, and I cannot say that it won me the affection of my children. In fact, from the day I started bringing home films like *Jack; Toys; Eddie; Corinna, Corrina; Jumpin' Jack Flash; Mr. Saturday Night; My Giant; My Stepmother Is an Alien; The Real McCoy; Cool World; Father's Day; The Telephone; The Getaway; Pret-à-Porter; Great Balls of Fire!; The Edge; Safe Passage; The Juror; Theodore Rex; Bogus;* and *To Wong Foo, Thanks for Everything, Julie Newmar*, I hardly ever saw my kids. The only time they would come into the family room when I was there was to make sure I hadn't yet rented *Stepmom*. If I'd ever rented *Stepmom*, I think they would have asked to be put up for adoption.

I knew that these were not good movies, just as I knew that not all whales deserved to be saved. But there was a larger moral issue: If watching *My Stepmother Is an Alien* or *The Juror* saved a single redwood or toucan, then it was worth watching them. Which is why I started lying about how bad they were. If I was in the video store and someone asked me to recommend a good film, I would pluck *Jack* or *Theodore Rex* off the shelf and insist that they give one of these vastly underrated, unjustly maligned little gems a whirl. Ultimately, I did not feel that my little white lies hurt anybody, because anybody who didn't already know what kind of film *Jack* or *Theodore Rex* was didn't deserve honest movie critiques. Moreover, I felt that my fibbing demonstrated how much I had evolved as a person. A year earlier, I had written a story for *Barron's* describing how I would tell people to buy *Pocahontas*, even though I had never seen it, because each sale would boost Disney's profits, and not only did I own stock in the company, but it published my books. Back then I was fibbing in the service of my own greed. Now I was fibbing in the service of virtue. And, of course, the spirit bear.

Another direct result of my spiritual conversion was that there were a lot fewer treats in the house. Before I made the decision to straighten up and fly right, I was the kind of father who was always surprising his kids with Eskimo Pies, Dove bars, ice-cream sandwiches. Now I came home laden with St. John's Wort Tortilla Chips, organic Cajun jerky, and strawberry kefir. The kids couldn't help but be annoyed. Still, there was only so far they could be pushed. Care for some Edensoy with your Cap'n Crunch, Gordon? *I don't think so.* How about if we just skip the Hot Pockets tonight and veg out on some rice-based cheese and organic Foney Baloney? *No way, José.* Shall we take some Newman's Own organic pretzels to the Mets game and give those char-broiled New York City soft pretzels a pass? *In a pig's eye.*

As was usually the case, my daughter was more accommodating on this issue than my son, and much more adventurous. That's because she wants to go to medical school and figured if it would keep her on my good side she didn't mind forcing down a couple of Tofu Wieners. One day she even agreed to accompany me to Union Square's famous greenmarket so I could buy a tub of fresh quark, which is impossible to find in the suburbs. We brought it home, she smeared some on a piece of bread, she ate it, she left the room, she never mentioned it again. Like I said: She wants to go to medical school. But my son was more like Jim Bowie at the Alamo. He'd rather take a bayonet than surrender his dignity. And eating bogus cheese slices made out of rice or lunch meat made out of soy or anything connected with whey—and then washing it down with organic wheatgrass—was his idea of humiliation.

I knew that I was making life difficult for my family. I knew that they hated the way I would root through the bathroom cabinets throwing away soaps and lotions manufactured by malevolent corporations. I could see the disappointment in their faces when I would come home laden with huge packages that they hoped were filled with Tastykakes but were brimming instead with organic nacho chips. I could tell how baffled they were about all that banjo music emanating from my stereo loudspeakers. And I knew that they felt betrayed when I would rent movies like *What Dreams May Come* and *My Giant* instead of *Con Air*.

Assistance in dealing with these problems came from a most unlikely source. One day I sat down to reread *Living Faith,* the eleventh book by Jimmy Carter. Two years earlier, I had ridiculed this volume in my acerbic book *Red Lobster, White Trash and the Blue Lagoon,* wondering how it was possible for God to love a man who let the prime interest rate reach the stratosphere, and who would write poetry like

> She'd smile, and birds would feel that they no longer
> had to sing, or it may be I failed
> to hear their song.

Now I approached Jimmy Carter from a totally new perspective. At long last, I realized that writing poetry helped the most virtuous ex-president, ex-czar, ex-imperator, ex-pasha the world has ever known to understand confusing issues he was wrestling with, and to communicate those feelings to others. One day, after reading his poem "To a Young Lawyer, My Son," which began with the words

> *One day I lashed out at my lawyer friends,*
> *and you were there*
> *to hear me ask why legal ways are often*
> *so unfair*

I decided to write a poem for my own son. It ran like this:

To a Young Dude

I know you think that I'm just a fool
But believe me, being cruel isn't cool.
You see, son, this is just my way of coping.
For minds are like parachutes—
They only work when open.

I know you'd rather be at a double feature
Than learning respect for the earth and all living creatures.
But give peace a chance, for I have a dream;
Dare to keep the CIA off drugs—we all live downstream.

Another practical tip I picked up from reading *Living Faith* involved apologies. At one point in the book, Jimmy explained how he patched up a conflict that had developed between him and his resolutely wonderful wife.

"Recently, after a particularly disturbing argument," he explained, "I decided that we should never let another day end with us angry with each other. I went to my wood shop and cut out a thin sheet of walnut, a little smaller than a bank check. I then carved on it: *Each evening, forever, this is good for an apology—or forgiveness—as you desire. Jimmy.*"

Because I have no carpentry skills, I simply took out one of my La Leche League checks and wrote an "apology" to my own son. It read:

"I'm sorry I rented *What Dreams May Come* and played that Sting record about the desaperecidos of Chile, or maybe it was Argentina, while you were trying to relax. You can either keep this check forever as a memento of your dad's affection, or cash it for $50 and buy a new video game. I know you will make the right decision."

Gord had hours of fun playing *Resident Evil II*.

My reading habits also changed as my search for secular sainthood continued. Where once I would burn the midnight oil reading depressing books by cynics like Samuel Beckett and P. J. O'Rourke, I would now pass the evenings reading one of Jimmy Carter's eleven works, or Ben & Jerry's *Double-Dip* or Anita Roddick's *Body and Soul* or *Sting: The Secret Life of Gordon Sumner* or *The Gita*, plus, of course, *Mother Jones, The Utne Reader*, and whatever happened to turn up inside my latest tube of Tom's of Maine toothpaste.

Laymen tend to think of such publications as being sappy and self-serving, but I did not find this to be the case. In fact, sometimes, when I needed a chuckle to buck me up I would read the amusing anecdotes on the backs of Newman's Own organic products. These were usually written by Paul Newman's daughter, Nell, who runs the organic division of the company. One described how "Papa" Newman developed the recipe for his salt & pepper rounds. Supposedly, he felt that putting salt on the roads during the winter was a bad idea and that pepper would make a better "condiment." Then he simply applied the same logic to his line of pretzels.

Oh, that Nell Newman. Such a cut-up.

Did I make compromises along the way in order to ensure family harmony? Of course I did. For while I eventually came to see that being a truly upstanding person was a full-time job and extended into every phase of one's existence, I also came to understand that there were times when you just had to back off and give it a rest. Sure, it annoyed me when my kids would ask me to buy them boxes of chocolates even though they knew that the candy company's record on toxic release inventory, as reported by the Council on Economic Priorities, was not good. But sometimes you just had to let kids be kids, and part of being a kid was stuffing your face with candy made by companies that had a dismal record on the toxic release inventory front. Land's sake, I know that's the way Huck and Tom would have reacted.

And yes, ideally, I would have liked to cancel my Con Edison account and sign up to receive green-certified, non–pollution-causing electricity from Green Mountain Energy Resources, especially since the company was offering a free subscription to *Mother Jones* if I ordered right away. But if I had gone through with my plan to switch electricity companies, my wife would have had me assassinated. A year earlier, when I'd switched my long-distance carrier from AT&T to MCI, AT&T had started sending us dunning notices for unpaid bills. Now I worried that the same thing might happen here. Already my wife was getting upset about the enormous amount of recyclable, environmentally sensitive junk mail we were getting. In the end, I decided to continue lighting my house with electricity supplied by a company I suspected was probably evil until the coast was clear.

For similar reasons, I decided to take a pass on ecologically conscious dry cleaning. One day, while surfing the tiny section of the Internet that is not devoted to genitalia, I discovered that the roughly $300 we spend on dry cleaning every year was inadvertently helping to "torture" the environment. I found this out when I logged onto the Cypress Plaza Cleaners website. Cypress Plaza Cleaners, located in Cypress, California, described itself as the neighborhood "green cleaners." Specifically, the company had altered the cleaning process in order to make it environmentally safe. This process allowed the firm to safely clean garments that were labeled "dry clean only" by using biodegradable soaps in specially computerized equipment. According to the website, "even wools, silks, linens, rayons, and cashmeres can be cleaned with quality equal or better than traditional dry cleaning, only without the unpleasant and unhealthful chemical odor of dry cleaning. In fact, our process usually makes whites whiter, works better on odor, and removes some stains more effectively than dry cleaning." The website listed a phone number, so I called and asked if I could get my dry cleaning done by mail.

The man who answered the phone said this would not be a problem, though he was obviously somewhat taken aback that I was prepared to ship my clothing all the way from New York and then have it shipped back each week UPS. But in the end, when I broached this subject to my wife, it was clear that this particular cause was not one we were likely to get into any time soon. Vegetarianism and general pro-environmental behavior and listening to Peter Gabriel records was one thing, but asking one's family to completely revolutionize its dry-cleaning philosophy was just too darned complicated.

Still, it irked me that my wife had so little interest in this daring innovation. Other women *did* have those types of sensitivities. How did I know? Because of information I found on the Internet. Whenever I had time to kill, I would try to educate myself about various issues by logging on to the Net and visiting socially conscious websites. One that caught my eye was run by an organization called Orbyss—"an electronic communication and publishing service for the environmental, vegetarian and animal rights communities" which provided "an environmentally sensitive, *paperless* system for information exchange, recruitment and activism." One of the most fascinating links was to something called the *Green Singles Newsletter.*

The *Green Singles Newsletter* provided a forum through which members of the environmental, vegetarian, and animal-rights communities, as well as other socially responsible singles who shared green values, could meet one another. Most of the people seemed to be the kinds of folks who reveled in the solitude of nature but would like to share the journey with a like-minded individual who was open to the new dimension of consciousness that an intimate relationship could bring. Not surprisingly, many were into holistic Shamanism, Chinese medicine, and herbology and wanted to connect with an earth or water sign whose favorite book was *The Gita*, whose hero was Ralph Nader, and whose most admired poet was Tagore. Wicans abounded, as did vegetarian Wicans and midwifery students interested in alternative healing arts, some of them seeking partners willing to devote their lives to slowing the destruction of this wondrous planet by political means and restoring the degraded part of it by physical labor, thus minimizing their ecological footprints. Nurturing relationships were important to them, as were astrology, healing therapies, and aquafitness. Needless to say, this was all quite new to me.

Reading through these want ads, I noticed several things. For starters, there was a great deal less emphasis upon deviant sex than in the classifieds I had seen in the *Village Voice*. Not once did I come across a personal reading

> Self-sufficient widowed Wiccan, vegetarian, nonsmoker, non-drinker, avid birder interested in spirituality, mother earth, alternative energy, log cabins. Seeking organic pagan partner who likes dances of universal peace, Science of Mind, haiku, hot wax, and bondage. No mustaches.

I am not saying that such people do not exist. I am only saying that if you are a self-sufficient organic pagan with a log cabin who likes hot candle wax and leather, the *Green Singles Newsletter* is probably not for you.

Another thing I gleaned from perusing these ads was that however serious my personal problems might seem to me, there were always other people who grazed in far less green pastures than I. For example, one day I read a personal listed in the *Green Singles* "Women Seeking Women" section, which had actually been written by a male. It ran like this:

> WEST VIRGINIA, rural: Hire apt, DWM, 50, 5' 9", 145 lbs. Modest, secure income. Effeminate male seeks femme LTR & pen-friends of like mind. Must believe in free amour. Must hate present-day Christian tyranny with a passion. No other racial or ethnic preferences. Interests: nature, green issues, religious & philosophical studies, poetry, music.

Let's face it, an effeminate male living in West Virginia who is seeking female free-amour pen pals who hate Christian tyranny, and who is trying to find them via the personal ads in the lesbian section of a green singles newsletter obviously has much bigger problems than me.

Finally, a very personal note. I suppose there is a time in every married man's life when he wonders where the road not taken would have taken him. This is not to say that he is unhappy with his current mate, but merely an admission that liaisons with other women might have turned out equally well, and perhaps even better. This is definitely the way I felt when I read the following ads in the "Women Seeking Men" section:

WASHINGTON, NW/BRITISH COLUMBIA: Gentle, strong, imperfect, DWF, 47, caring mother, (independent 16, 20 yrs.) 5' 4", HWP. Enviro-friendly, healthy, vegetarian, country lifestyle. Healing-Arts Practitioner. Artisan. Well-balanced—innately spiritual. Humanitarian. Lover of: laughter, wildness, solitude, Sacredness, spontaneity, Adventure, home—extended family, intimacy, books, music, dancing, arts, Alternative Healing, Human Potential. Seeking communicative, wise, grounded, NS man to create deeply loving LTR, WR.

Gosh, witchy woman, where were you when I needed you?

14908-KOREA, Seoul: Grounded in the earth sign of Virgo, yet Independent, High-spirited…Visionary…a woman bound for adventure and any contemplative, spiritual path that includes a hot tub…40-something, slender, said to be VERY pleasant to look at! A Tibetan Buddhist and doctor of Oriental Medicine, I am a high-profile executive working internationally. I have a passion for film, photography, writing, cats and nature. I long to grow old with a man who possesses and expresses wit and humor first, and charm, articulation, brilliance and creativity second. A meditation practice is preferred, and one capable of writing that is inspired, humorous, clever, original, insightful a Big plus (I have to travel a lot!).

Had we but world enough and time!

And finally:

MAINE: Capricornian musician, masseuse, fiber artist, 44, 5' 8",
135 lbs., deeply spiritual, intuitively inclined, pretty, simply
amused, fascinated by dreams, earthly rhythms, inner growth,
travel, mothering, lover of beauty, animals, peach juice, Celtic
music, organics, living things. ISO male complementary counter-
part with strong sense of self and the interconnectedness of life
to share this earth journey with warmth, kindness, wisdom, and
mirth.

The one that got away.

7 • The Frugal

Philanthropist

One true thing I had learned from my study of the history of altruism was that there was more than one way to skin the philanthropic cat. There was "noisy philanthropy," as defined by Paul Newman and Ben & Jerry, where virtuous merchants used the labels on their edible products to promote worthy causes or remind people how much money they had given away. Then there was quiet philanthropy, as practiced by people like Frank Sinatra, who would quietly pick up the tab for people who were down on their luck. There was also belligerent philanthropy, where the well-heeled deliberately bankrolled certain causes because they knew it would piss certain people off, and passive philanthropy, where affluent types blithely wrote checks to important organizations but let them do all the heavy lifting. Other categories one need not go into here include gynophilanthropy (the exclusive support of women's causes), retrophilanthropy (support for causes that have gone out of fashion), simiaphilanthropy (support of species one step down on the evolutionary scale from humans), and salsaphilanthropy (support for impoverished individuals based in the Caribbean). Finally, there is the type of philanthropy I happen to practice, which is champagne philanthropy on a beer pocketbook.

Let me explain how my philosophy took root. As the days and weeks rolled past, and more and more of my income was devoured by RAKs and SABs, I realized that I was going to have to keep a closer watch on my hemp-based checkbook. Slowly but surely, I began to develop a world view that fused concern for the planet and the well-being of my fellow man with a sharper sense of fiscal responsibility. In short, I found myself evolving into a frugal philanthropist. Not a cheapskate, by any stretch of the imagination, but a person who kept a tighter rein on the purse strings.

A case in point: the rain forest. One morning, while reviewing my moral index, I realized that to date I hadn't done anything for the primeval wilderness that is the mother of us all. I'd been so busy with other projects that I'd completely forgotten that one of our most precious resources was being systematically destroyed by predatory miners, perfidious loggers, corrupt government officials, unscrupulous toucan smugglers, depraved poachers, and assorted henchpersons.

As luck would have it, the Rainforest Foundation was holding its Ninth Annual Benefit Concert at Carnegie Hall, with performers ranging from Sting to Elton John to James Taylor to Don Henley, but also including less obvious environmentalists such as Tony Bennett and Billy Joel. Ticket prices were scaled from $100 to $350. This was pretty hefty, but I figured that if I could get this concert out of the way, the rain forest and I would be even-steven for the rest of the year, leaving me free to concentrate on causes of greater personal interest. But when I called Carnegie Hall to buy tickets, lo and behold, the only ones still on sale were partial-view numbers at $250 and $350 apiece. There was no way I could swing $350 for a partial view of Don Henley, not with the Spirit

Bear still on the ropes out there. So I placated my conscience by eating lunch at the Rainforest Café and buying some Ben & Jerry's Rainforest Crunch, promising myself to catch the genuine rain forest on the rebound. Agreed, it was not the ideal way to help save the planet. But it was a lot better that eating a morally neutral meal at Wendy's and then scarfing down a pint of Häagen-Dazs. The truth is, I cared about the rain forest. I just didn't care as much as some other people.

The key point to remember here is that when you set out to be a virtuous person, it is essential not to spread yourself too thin. No matter how important certain causes may seem, some are more important than others, and every ounce of energy and every dollar that is devoted to one cause inexorably detracts from another. Thus, as my voyage of self-renewal gathered momentum, it was essential that I begin to prioritize. I had the strength to become a lacto vegetarian, but not the strength to become an all-out vegetarian. Human rights were more important than animal rights. Whales were more important than manatees or, for that matter, Spirit Bears. Poor black children were more important than lesbians, but lesbians were more important than gay men because they were women, and women have babies, and men of quality support women's equality. If you see what I'm driving at.

One of the great risks a newly good person runs is being seduced by the tchotchkes of virtue—the shade-grown coffee, the soy-based checkbook covers, the Spirit Bear tote bag—and not concentrating on what really matters: making the world a better place to live in, because good planets are hard to find. It was my sense of moral prioritization that prevented me from executing a number of purchases I would otherwise have loved to make. For example, I spent hours and hours paging through the Pax Organica catalog (cover printed on hemp; 25 percent hemp rag and 75 percent pre-consumer recycled fiber [textile waste]), thinking about sending away for organic cotton tights for my wife. But spending $11.50 on organic tights (plus $4.50 S & H) was money better spent on buying the new record by Sting, which would give him extra cash to help save the rain forest with Alec Baldwin and Kim Basinger. Sure, those tights would have made a nice organic yuletide stocking stuffer. But they were certainly not essential.

Gradually, I developed a game plan for my new approach to life. Here, in full regalia, is the basic play book for effective Frugal Philanthropy:

1. **Don't be afraid to send singles.** In one day, I sent contributions to the Glaucoma Foundation, Guiding Eyes for the Blind, and the Make-a-Wish Foundation. I sent a single dollar to the first two and $2 to the second. The next day, I sent singles to the Nature Conservancy and Farm Sanctuary, an organization that campaigns for the rights of downed animals. This did not mean that the beneficiaries of the Make-a-Wish Foundation could not make a wish. It simply meant that they had to keep their wishes modest.

2. **Don't go overboard.** If you've already sent $20 to Greenpeace, you're pretty well clear on the marine biology front and don't need to send anything to the Center for Marine Conservation. If you want to send a couple of bucks, feel free. But don't feel that you have to. Let somebody else carry the ball for a change.

3. **Prioritize your contributions for maximum environmental impact.** This is a lesson I had to learn the hard way. Early in my transformation, I sent a check to Defenders of Wildlife, which covered the adoption of a wolf. A few weeks later, probably because I was now on all the prominent animal adoption mailing lists, I received a letter from the World Wildlife Fund asking me to send $15 and adopt a tiger. Tigers are obviously a much more imperiled species than wolves, so I wrote the check right away. But in retrospect I wish that I had curtailed my lupine largess and spent the cash on tigers instead, if only because adopting a tiger is an act of incontestable virtue, whereas the verdict is still out on wolves, who are certainly no big hit with farmers. Whenever possible, try to orient your generosity toward beneficiaries that provide you with the greatest moral and public relations reward (tigers, Kurds, the rain forest), and stay away from the grayer

areas (wolves, lab animals, homeless communists). As a rule of thumb, before selecting an endangered species to help protect, check to see if Judy Collins or the Paul Winter Consort has ever recorded an album using their mating calls in the background. Sorry, Mr. Spirit Bear; you don't make the cut.

4. **Whenever possible, try to practice RAKs that don't cost anything.** If the hapless, illiterate immigrant at your local video store can't find *Predator II* because he doesn't understand that the film is not a comedy, go into the stacks and locate it for him. Offer newspapers you've finished reading to fellow commuters. And carry around up-to-date schedules for trains and buses you don't even ride, so that if somebody needs to know when the next conveyance is coming through, you can tell them. A totally unexpected gesture, and just really, really nice.

5. **Practice RAKs on the road.** One night while staying at a comfy, mid-range hotel in Los Angeles, I went into the bathroom and read one of those eco-hints that have become so prevalent in hostelries these days. You know, the little notes asking guests to reuse their towels because that way hotels do not have to waste our precious aquatic resources doing the laundry. Well, this time I went one better than the ordinary one-towel guy. Instead of taking a daily bath during my three-day stay, I would purge the grime and sweat from my body every morning by using the hotel pool. Sure, it was a tad nippy in an outdoor pool in late February, but the overriding rush I got from my selfless gesture helped to shake off the shivers. Obviously, this is not the ideal approach to bathing: The chlorine mats your hair, and halfway through my appearance on *The Late Late Show* my skin started to feel kind of itchy. But this seemed like a small price to pay if it would keep earth in the balance. Seriously, if not now, when? If not us, whom? Hey, we all live downstream.

6. **Wherever possible, keep your eyes peeled for two-fers.** When you give a dollar to a bag person, you are only helping

the poor. But when you give it to the deaf woman who sells pencils on the subway, you are not only helping the poor, but you are also helping the deaf poor, and quite frequently, the multiculturally deaf poor. Unless homeless people can present some evidence that your contribution is a two-tiered, value-added gesture, keep your money to yourself.

7. **Wait till things go on sale.** Since he launched Newman's Own in the early 1980s, Paul Newman has given away $90 million to more than one thousand groups. One reason he has been able to give away so much money is because his products are so expensive and he doesn't seem to give away cents-off coupons. So my advice is to wait until they go on sale before buying them.

Let me supply another fine example of a two-fer. On Sunday, May 2, 1999, the American Cancer Society sponsored a Dog Walk Against Cancer in Riverside Park, New York City. Registration was $20. The very same day, the SPCA of Westchester sponsored a Dog Walkathon in Katonah, New York. Registration involved no cost. On the surface, this would seem to be a layup for the Frugal Philanthropist: Go with the free event.

But when you scratched beneath the surface, the choice was less than obvious. The dog walk in New York was intended to raise money for the fight against both animal and human cancers. The dog walk in Katonah was only intended to raise money—through sponsors—for the SPCA. Because the dog walk in Manhattan benefited both humans and animals, it meant that I didn't have to do anything else of a philanthropic nature for the next two weeks, which would free up time for extra work, which could be used to earn more money, which I could then use to write more and even larger checks to other worthy causes. Thus, even though the Dog Walk cost $20 more than the event held in Katonah, it freed up a much larger amount of moral currency.

There was more. On my way to the Dog Walk Against Cancer, it occurred to me that since the American Cancer Society already had my $20, it wasn't necessary to actually attend the dog walk. Though a friend had agreed to lend me her dog for the day, she cautioned that I would have to take the dog all the way uptown in a taxi and that he would probably puke all over the cab. A trip from the Lower East Side to the Upper West Side was going to set me back approximately $15, and I was probably going to make life miserable for some hard-working immigrant who would have to spend the rest of the day driving around in a puke-stained cab. This would not only make his life horrible from the olfactory point of view but would result in fewer tips. Thus, my original act of generosity toward dogs and cancer victims would have the unintended but no less harmful effect of reducing an immigrant's income and very possibly increasing Third World alienation toward well-heeled but spoiled white people who could afford to engage in RAKs and SABs because they didn't have to clean up the dog vomit.

In the end, I decided that it made more sense to skip the Dog Walk altogether and spend the day engaged in other RAKs. One of these was to attend the Dog Toy Drive in Tompkins Square Park. The Toy Drive was intended both to collect toys and to raise money to buy toys for dogs confined to animal shelters. I took a quick gander at the items that had been collected so far—a pretty shoddy assortment—and marched right up the street to a conveniently located pet shop to purchase a sturdy, shiny dog toy. Another $11.95 down the hopper of virtue. When I returned to the park, I asked one of the event organizers if similar drives were ever held to collect toys for dogs languishing in Third World animal shelters. She told me that she doubted it, noting that the correct term for Third World abandoned dogs is "dinner."

One final note: This Sunday excursion clearly fell into *both* categories of RAKs and SABs, as I hate dogs.

Another good example of the Frugal Philanthropist at work was the April 24, 1999, "Millions for Mumia" rally held in my native Philadelphia. Mumia Abu-Jamal is the African-American journalist sentenced to death in 1982 for the murder of Philadelphia police officer Daniel Faulkner the previous year. In the interim, *l'affaire* Mumia had become a cause célèbre, with many people believing that he had been railroaded by a white judge and a predominantly white jury in a city that has a vast African-American population. His supporters ranged from Susan Sarandon to Alice Walker to Michael Stipe to David Mamet to Whoopi Goldberg to the Beastie Boys. In San Francisco, mayor Willie Brown had declared a day in Mumia's honor. Several cities, including Detroit, Michigan, and Cambridge, Massachusetts, had passed resolutions demanding a retrial. French president Jacques Chirac —a known conservative—had come out in his defense, as had political figures in Germany, South Africa, and even Belgium. Perhaps the single greatest measure of Mumia's stature, as *Mother Jones* had reported, was the fact that at least one rally in his defense had taken place in Oslo. Since this was the first time in the 20th century that the Norwegian people had had anything to say about anything, Abu-Jamal must surely have taken comfort from this utterly unexpected Scandinavian endorsement.

On April 24, 1999, a rally in Mumia's honor and defense was held outside City Hall in downtown Philadelphia. Needless to say, I was one of the thousands in attendance. My reasons for going to the Mumia rally were varied, but primarily the event fulfilled my essential criteria for maximizing efficiency in the performance of RAKs and SABs. One, it enabled me to demonstrate solidarity with the African-American community. Two, it allowed me to lend support to political prisoners everywhere. Three, it enabled me to register my opposition to capital punishment. Fourth, because it doesn't take that long to demonstrate my solidarity with the African-American community, lend support to political prisoners everywhere, and register my opposition to capital punishment, it freed up an entire afternoon to have lunch with an old friend and visit several of Philadelphia's lovely museums. I arrived at the rally at 10:30, signed a few petitions, chatted with some plucky old leftists, and then punched out, right around lunchtime.

My afternoon was spent visiting the Rodin Museum, an exhibition of unusual gallstones at the Academy of Medicine and Physicians, and the small but charming Goya exhibit at the Philadelphia Museum of Art. I should also note that I did all this on the cheap, bypassing the normal $76 round-trip Amtrak fare to Philadelphia by taking New Jersey Transit from Penn Station to Trenton ($19 round-trip) and then catching a local Southeastern Pennsylvania Transit Authority train from Trenton to 30th Street Station ($10 round-trip) in Philly. Thus, all told,

I got in a full morning of social activism and a long afternoon of cultural immersion for $29, plus lunch, museum admissions, taxis, and tips. This was frugal philanthropy at its very best.

The question can legitimately be raised whether I would have made the same trip in support of Mumia Abu-Jamal had the rally been held in Wheeling, West Virginia, or Knoxville, Tennessee. The answer is probably no. Had the Mumia rally involved a larger expenditure of cash to visit a municipality boasting fewer cultural resources, I probably would have stayed in New York and protested the alleged mistreatment of elephants by Ringling Brothers and Barnum & Bailey or the Giuliani administration's sinister plan to auction off the sites of 122 community gardens or eaten in a Tibetan restaurant in support of the Dalai Lama. I do not think, however, that this makes me any less a person. Moreover, I suspect that the organizers of major protest marches understand that the average person, no matter how upstanding, is not interested in attending rallies in cities that do not have good restaurants, fine museums, or revitalized seaport areas. All kidding aside, folks, when was the last time they held a big protest in Worcester, Massachusetts, or Lawrence, Kansas?

Before we go any further, let me 'fess up that I didn't really enjoy the rally that much because the organizers kept blasting rap music and I find rap to be culturally noninclusive, misogynistic, aggressive, and often downright mean. Because I had evolved into an *It Takes A Whole Village* T-shirt kind of guy, I was disturbed by the palpable negativity at the gathering. Luckily, just to be on the safe side, I had packed my *Columbus Didn't Discover the New World...He Invaded It* T-shirt, which I quickly switched to when it became obvious that this was not a *Random Acts of Senseless Beauty* kind of crowd.

But I didn't feel terribly comfortable wearing the Columbus shirt either, because I really couldn't see how the conquistadors were that much worse than the bloodthirsty Aztecs and the repressive Incas. Moreover, if Columbus hadn't discovered, invaded, whatever the New World, I'd probably be working the night shift in some bog in West

Cork instead of practicing RAKs in the City That Loves You Back. I'll level with you: The Path of Righteousness was replete with moral ambiguities.

A second reservation had to do with the way the event was organized. Frankly, I didn't care for the way the communists, the socialists, the Native Americans, the lesbians, the antiwar people, and even the vegans had pile-driven their way into this protest. The rally was supposed to raise global consciousness about the plight of a man widely believed to be unjustly incarcerated. Relevant themes included capital punishment, police brutality, the inherent racism of the American jurisprudence system. This had nothing to do with Cuba, Kosovo, Iraq, vegetarianism, or Wounded Knee. The grab-bag, one-size-fits-all nature of the protest really annoyed me, which is one reason I didn't hang around very long. This is one message I would like to impart to people interested in finding out how to be good: If you're not enjoying a protest, saddle up and ride. It's important that you come, sure, but it's not that important that you stay. As Ben & Jerry once said: *If it's not fun, why do it?*

Aesthetically, the Mumia rally also failed to please. Basically, this is because dissident fashion hasn't changed much since the great protest days of the 1960s. The aging white leftists still wear Mao caps and inappropriate fatigues and too many buttons and too much ineptly groomed facial hair. And the black guys all dress like Bob Marley. Moreover, the cops never get down and dirty. I think that rallies like Millions for Mumia are good training grounds for young people who do not have any experience in heavy-duty protesting. But without tear gas and mounted horsemen wielding billy clubs, these events lack drama. They are the political equivalent of Triple A ball: a good place to learn the ropes, but certainly not The Show.

I got a very clear sense of what a down-market protest this was when one of the organizers introduced the 28th Elder of what I believe was the Piscataway Nation and the chieftain climbed up on stage and said that the whole Mumia trial was invalid because the judicial proceedings had taken place on land stolen from its rightful owners. I had to admire the jesuitical subtleties of his argument, but the bald truth is I couldn't help feeling that if the Native-American community really cared that much about Mumia Abu-Jumal one way or the other, they would have sent out some heavy hitters like Crazy Horse's grandson or Cochise's great-nephew or Chief Joseph of the Nez Perce IV. The Pequot and the Piscataway were terrific nations in their own right, but for the rally to muster some true aboriginal buzz you really needed some Apaches, Dakota Sioux, or Iroquois added to the mix.

But my biggest reservation of all was that I didn't honestly believe that Mumia was innocent. I don't think that many other people did, either, because the event was pretty poorly attended. After all, even *Mother Jones,* my newfound moral compass, had admitted that Mumia was a less than ideal poster guy for the anti–capital-punishment movement. Mumia fell into the same general category as Tawana Brawley and Rigoberta Menchú: public figures who had achieved the almost impossible task of becoming mythological figures while still alive, even though the exploits they were being mythologized for never actually happened. But hey, did anyone seriously believe that Hercules had cleaned the Augean stables by diverting a river? In any case, the one true thing I had learned as the Frugal Philanthropist was to make the best of a bad situation and to take out of an unsatisfactory experience as much as I could get. Specifically, I used my visit to Philadelphia to finally get to the bottom of the whole *Una Puebla Unida* thing, which had been bothering me for months.

As the reader will recall from an earlier chapter where I tried to get my Message!Checks emblazoned with my own personal slogan, there has always been a soft spot in my heart for the *Una Puebla Unida* rallying cry, because we used to chant it together back in the Movement Days when Dylan was still Divine. Though I could not recall specifically whether the slogan referred to the Venceremos Brigade, Cesar Chavez, or that Salvador Allende brouhaha, it had long been my favorite clarion call and I never felt that a protest or rally was complete unless I got to sing it. But the sad truth is, I never actually learned to chant it correctly. An elitist snob, I had mastered French at an early age, and could get along nicely in Italian, but for one reason or another I had never learned Spanish. Because of this, I never learned whether we were supposed to be shouting "Un Puebla Unida Jamas Seras Vencida" or "Un Pueblo Unido Jamas Sera Vencido" or what. In my defense, back in the

Days of Rage when we were offing the pigs and kicking out the jams because they had the guns but we had the numbers, a lot of us didn't have time for such linguistic delicacies. Also, we were smoking so much dope and the heat was coming down on us with so much tear gas that in the end we didn't know whether we were part of the solution or part of the problem. It's also fair to say that in an era where you could be in my dreams if I could be in yours, nobody really cared if we were speaking Spanish correctly as long as we had LBJ and Tricky Dick on the run.

Comforted by the knowledge that I had not in fact kicked out my final jam, I viewed the Millions for Mumia Rally as a gold-plated opportunity to finally get this Una Puebla Unida thing nailed down once and for all. So I started wandering around Dilworth Plaza, across from Philadelphia's weird, neo-Gothic city hall, looking for old Movement people who could help me resolve this cultural conundrum. I must have asked a half dozen grizzled veterans whether it was "Una Puebla" or "Un Pueblo," but nobody seemed to know. Amazingly, a lot of the old-timers—commies, socialists, guys in Greek fisherman caps—acted like they'd never even heard the expression. This made me really nervous. Nobody who'd been there when we fucked with the Man back in the days of the Strawberry Statement, when everything was everything, could possibly have not heard that trusty old slogan. So I strongly suspected that these so-called Movement vets were either fakes, parvenus, arrivistes, Johnny-come-latelies, fellow-travelers, agents provocateurs, informants, stool pigeons, or undercover cops. That or Trotskyites—always a huge pain in the ass. As the afternoon wore on, I became more selective about who I talked to, fearing that they might have hidden cameras in their bifocals and were taking my picture for the CIA. Hey, it wouldn't be the first time. I was *there* when we levitated the Pentagon.

Finally I ran into a German woman who said that her husband spoke a little Spanish. He told me that "puebla" was the Spanish word for "village," while "pueblo" was the Spanish word for "people." He also said that he was from Macedonia. When I asked him whether it was true that Alexander the Great had conspired with his mother to murder his father Philip II, he said he didn't know anything about Alexander the Great. Since Alexander the Great and his father Philip are the only Macedonians anyone has ever heard of, I no longer believed that this character was a native of Macedonia. And I certainly didn't trust his command of the Spanish language.

In fact, I was just about ready to give up on the whole project and buy myself a biography of Che Guevara or a cheap Spanish grammar when I spied a sprightly young woman carrying a huge sign reading, YA BASTA!!!

"Does that mean 'Enough already'?" I inquired, since I knew that *basta* meant "enough" in Italian, a cognate of the noble Castilian idiom.

"Yes," she replied with a big, left-of-center smile.

"I guess you're Spanish-speaking then?"

"Yes," she replied.

"Well, maybe you can help me. I've always wondered whether the rallying cry 'Una Puebla Unida Jamas Seras Vencida' is the correct way to say it in Spanish."

"No," she replied helpfully. "*Pueblo* is the word for 'village' or 'people.' So it's *Un pueblo...*"

"*Un pueblo,*" I repeated.

"*Unido...*"

"*Unido...*"

"*Ha-más...*"

"*Ha-más...*" I echoed.

"*Será vencido.*"

"*Será vencido.*"

"*Un pueblo unido jamás será vencido.*"

"*Un pueblo unido jamás será vencido!*" I repeated triumphantly. Then I was on my way. My outing had been successful and now it was time to grab the train back to New York and attend a fiftieth birthday party for a dear old friend—another senseless act of random kindness.

But hold on to your hats, dear reader, because RAKs-wise, I was just getting warmed up.

8 . Capitol Gains

As the weeks zipped past, I found myself feeling better and better about the person I had become, or was in the process of becoming. That person was someone who recognized that Columbus had not discovered the New World (as if!) but had merely invaded it, someone who did not let his friends vote Republican, someone who understood that we all live downstream —though some further downstream than others—and finally, someone who ate nothing with a face, much less an ass.

Inevitably, my odyssey of emotional self-repackaging prompted me to establish my own small-scale, grassroots philanthropic foundation that I hoped would bring bliss and soul-balm to complete strangers, yet do so in a completely aleatory fashion. The foundation was called Dolci for Dissidents, and its mission was to supply creamy Italian desserts in a nonpartisan fashion to the people who camp out in Lafayette Square directly across the street from the White House protesting a wide number of social inequities. By doing so, Dolci would enable these watchdogs of democracy to keep the chimes of freedom burning while a nation of sheep were lulled into the dark sleep of reason.

I decided to deliver creamy Italian pastries—specifically cannoli—to the protesters across the street from the White House because I knew that no one else was likely ever to have thought of it. Unlike that flamboyant, mediagenic tree lady who has taken up residence in a one-thousand-year-old California redwood to protest logging or Nelson Mandela or Susan Sarandon, the protesters in Lafayette Square had never been viewed as fashionable or cool or important or even likable. If people thought about them at all, they viewed them as being some-what pathetic. This is because there is a basic belief in this society that people who camp out overnight for things are insane, unless the Yankees or Springsteen are involved. Obviously, this is considered even more true of people who camp out for years at a time. I should point out that during my freshman year in college I did once camp out all night to protest the war in Biafra, but I only did it to meet girls. I did in fact meet a fantastic girl, but the Biafrans lost the war, and by the time the next meaningful all-night vigil came to pass I already had a new, fully functional girlfriend and had turned mildly right wing.

To me, the protesters in Lafayette Square were the late-20th century equivalent of Christ's samaritans, low-rent outcasts whose needs paled before those of the Kurds, the giant sequoia, or the Spirit Bear. An unexpected donation of cannoli, I strongly suspected, could mitigate their pathos. But the most important component of my particular brand of philanthropy was its random quality, for quietly, at the micro-level, I was seeking to spread the word that entirely unexpected good things could happen to people if they just happened to be in the right place at the right time. Ultimately, this would tie in with my burgeoning pantheistic creed that love is all around and that the amount you give is equal to the amount you make.

Due to a lack of planning, Dolci for Dissidents was not the rip-roaring success I had anticipated. The big problem was in finding those darned dolci. Washington, unlike New York City, is not the sort of place where you can just amble down the street and happen upon a well-stocked Italian bakery at every corner. Washington is more of an Au Bon Pain kind of town. This I discovered on my arrival one fine May afternoon, when I checked in with a friend who I had enlisted to help me find the cannoli. My friend, who lives in suburban Virginia, said that she had spent the entire previous day on the phone trying to track down a bakery that baked fresh cannoli every day. Sadly, her efforts had not been rewarded. In fact, if she had only bothered to call me, I would have bought the cannoli in New York and brought them down on the Metroliner. But no.

First my friend tried a number of Italian bakeries. No luck. Then she called Dean & DeLuca, an upscale purveyor of fine gourmandise. The manager said the store didn't sell them anymore, but that they could special-order them. Next she went on the Internet to find a list of bakeries in the Washington area that might bake cannoli. These ranged from the Pastry Institute to The Sunspot Coffee and Bakery to Sam's Donuts. All told, she contacted fifteen different establishments. None of them sold cannoli.

Eventually, someone recommended the Sutton Place Gourmet, located on Massachusetts Avenue. Here she had mixed results. The establishment said that it did not regularly bake cannoli, but could special-order them. However, in order to have them by Tuesday, they would have had to have been ordered by the previous Friday. Nothing speaks more eloquently of Washington's inherently Ostrogothic character than this anecdote.

Because I had a bad case of the flu, had just spent the weekend with my mother, and had important business to conduct the next day, I wanted to make an early night of it. But since I so desperately wanted the initial gesture by Dolci for Dissidents to be a success, I took a cab up to Georgetown and prowled the streets for several hours gunning for some fresh cannoli. Mission impossible. Though I did ferret out some fruit tarts, petits fours, and tiramisu, I could not actually unearth anything that would officially qualify as dolci. Worse still, there was no mini-bar or refrigerator in my no-frills hotel where I could have stored the goodies, so even if I'd stumbled upon a trove of the desserts, they would have spoiled overnight. And by this point, I wasn't all that thrilled about purchasing ostensibly Neapolitan pastries in a town where nobody even knew what a cannoli was. They might be inedible. Eventually, I decided that the best approach was to come back the next morning and buy the closest thing to dolci available, then head over to Lafayette Park.

Unfortunately, when I returned to the hotel that evening, I realized that my appointments calendar was completely booked up. Breakfast at 8:30 with a colleague. Coffee with a second colleague at 10:15. And then an important public speaking engagement at 12:30. That didn't leave much time to be screwing around. So the next morning, I rose at 6:30 A.M. and strolled off toward the White House, resigned to improvising as best I could.

The closest thing to dolci I could find along the way were a couple of packages of Krispy Kreme doughnuts, which I purchased from a Pakistani street vendor. Although Krispy Kremes were considerably less elegant than the savory delights I had originally set my sights on, they were infinitely more appealing than Drake's Cakes or Devil Dogs. Moreover, back up north Krispy Kremes had attained a certain cachet in recent years: Even the krusty old *New York Times* had devoted a story to the opening of the first Krispy Kreme establishment in Manhattan in 1997. So I did not feel like I was phoning it in by delivering the doughnuts to whomever I found protesting in Lafayette Square.

The person I found protesting in Lafayette Square shortly after daybreak was a relatively handsome bearded man with quite a pleasant demeanor. He looked like Brad Pitt after about five and a quarter years in Tibet.

"How do you feel about some Krispy Kremes this morning?" I asked, sliding a package of chocolate-covered mini-doughnuts out of my paper bag.

"Sounds great," he replied.

"My name is Joe Queenan and I represent an organization called Dolci for Dissidents which supplies dessert-oriented materials in a non-partisan fashion to political dissidents who are keeping the embers of freedom glowing," I announced, pointing to my colorful, canary yellow shirt with its sophisticated black lettering. The man said that was a good thing.

The beneficiary of my matinal munificence now identified himself as Troy and explained that he was a member of the Peace Park Antinuclear Vigil, which had been operating continuously in Lafayette Square since June 3, 1981. He said that Concepcion, the woman who usually ran the operation, was taking a break but would be back soon. I asked if Concepcion actually lived in her little enclosure in the park and he said that she did. I then asked how she went about doing things like taking a shower, and he said that the group had taken over an abandoned building not far away and had a fully working bathroom there. The group also had its own website.

I was happy that Concepcion had a shower to use, though it crossed my mind that a sister organization called Doccia for Dissidents, which would allow dissidents to use the shower in my hotel room, was another option I might consider at some point in the future. Actually, my mind was already racing ahead to a double-barreled RAK & SAB: an organization called Dolci AND Doccia for Dissidents, which would invite protesters into a fancy hotel for dessert, and then let them use the shower. It definitely had possibilities. Though it's probably only fair to point out that as Troy and I wrapped up our conversation, I noticed that he had not actually opened the Krispy Kreme package. This made me feel less upset about falling down on the cannoli assignment. I think that Troy would have suspected that the cannoli were poisoned and had been sent over by shadowy mob land figures who had some vague connection with Jack Ruby. Krispy Kremes, shrink-wrapped, were far less ominous, so in the fullness of time he might see fit to open them.

One question that might be raised at this juncture is how this two-day jaunt to our nation's capital coalesced with my identity as the Frugal Philanthropist. Especially since I took the pricey Metroliner. In fact, my transportation had been paid for by the United States Department of Agriculture. This was another excellent example of philanthropic piggybacking: using the opportunity to do one good deed as an opportunity to do a second, safe in the knowledge that the expenses for the latter would be covered by the proceeds from the former. Though I must admit that the first good deed only came about after considerable grappling with disconcerting moral issues.

Let me explain. Back in the fall of 1998, long before my crisis of conscience, I had accepted an invitation from an old friend, who worked as a publicist for the United States Department of Agriculture, to give a speech to a group of his colleagues in Washington, D.C. All of the people attending the "Communicating Creatively" luncheon at the White House Conference Center were government employees and most of them worked for the USDA. At the time I agreed to deliver the speech, I had no moral qualms about the group I was addressing, as the USDA seemed like a perfectly decent, honorable, and even likable organization. It wasn't as if I was giving a *pro bono* speech to the CIA.

But as the date of the engagement approached, I began to feel seriously conflicted. One afternoon, I received a flyer from the American Anti-Vivisection Society condemning the USDA for its stand on the treatment of lab animals. According to the AAVS, the USDA, an organization I had always viewed as essentially helpful and generally harmless, was violating the spirit of the Animal Welfare Act by deeming rats, mice, and birds "non-animals," and allowing scientific researchers to subject them to horrible experimentation. The flyer said that the USDA knew perfectly well that when Congress passed the act it wanted these creatures protected, but for some reason the agency chose to ignore the will of the people's duly elected representatives. The AAVS was now seeking 35,000 public comments to support its position and persuade the USDA to change its policy.

You can imagine what a pickle this put me in! Here I thought I was doing an old friend a good turn by giving a pro bono speech (travel expenses only, but no honorarium, if you can imagine that) to an agency most people admired, and now I found out that the USDA was directly implicated in the cruel and unusual death of millions of lab animals. What on earth was I to do?

At first I tried to take the cowardly way out by calling my friend, complaining of chronic migraines, and asking him to find a substitute speaker. But he said that it was already too late, that the programs had already been printed up, and that it would be impossible to find a speaker as awesomely talented as me, who was willing to work for so little, especially on such short notice. (He did not actually say that I was awesomely talented, but it was clearly implied.) Whatever my other failings, I do not go back on my word, especially to someone who had helped me at an earlier point in my career (one of my first published stories was a *Wall Street Journal* op-ed piece about bizarre, amusing, or just plain strange USDA programs). But at the same time, I genuinely believed that my appearance at this venue would demonstrate that I lacked the courage of my convictions, and that the first time push came to shove, I would allow myself to be shoved.

The imbroglio was fraught with moral, ethical, zoological, and avian nuances. On the one hand, I did not care much about scientific experiments on rats, because rats were responsible for the Black Death, and it seemed to me that a certain amount of biological retribution was a cross they would simply have to bear. In the vernacular of the masses, what goes around comes around. But mice were a cuddly, diffident breed who did not deserve to be lumped in with their sinister rodent kin, and as an avid new drinker of shade-grown coffee I recognized that birds were my bewinged soul mates. So I could not act as if I didn't care what happened to them. It would have been hypocritical to drink shade-grown, pro-ornithological coffee—the official beverage of the San Francisco Zoo, by the way—at home, and then tickle the ribs of birds' sworn enemies on the road. No, I had to take a stand.

The situation resolved itself in an unexpected but wholly satisfactory fashion. One morning I read in the *New York Post* that the USDA was investigating "elephant abuse" at Ringling Bros. and Barnum & Bailey's circus. According to the *Post*, a former circus employee had filed a five-page affidavit alleging that elephants had been savagely beaten by their keepers and were kept in chains for days on end. Needless to say, the circus denied these allegations. This did not matter, at least not to me. What mattered was that the USDA was taking the initiative in investigating the alleged abuses. And because elephants are an endangered species and occupy a much higher position on the evolutionary seeding chart than rats, mice, and birds—with the obvious exception of snail darters, condors, and bald eagles—the USDA's vigilance deserved to be honored. One way of honoring it was by giving a pro bono (travel expenses only, no fee!) speech to a group of its employees.

In no way, shape, or form was I absolving the USDA of its complicity in the mistreatment of lab animals. No siree, bob. I am proud to say that on the day that I gave the speech, which dealt with the use of show tunes such as "If Ever I Should Leave You" to induce cell phone junkies to stop annoying their fellow passengers with their studiously unnecessary calls on the Metroliner, I digressed from my humorous presentation for a few moments to chastise the assembled USDA publicists for the agency's cavalier attitude toward lab animals. Specifically, I said that everything in the universe has a function, even Michael Bolton, and that this was also true of rats. But that wasn't the way the USDA saw things. Oh, no! At this point, I announced that I was onto their little scam, then demanded that they do everything in their power to make the USDA reverse its heartless policy and confer on rats, mice, and birds the same legal safeguards as more sympathetic, Disney-like creatures. Then I went back to talking about show tunes and cell phone abusers.

How did the audience react? I guess they thought I was joking. They seemed to be waiting for a punch line that never came. This did not bother me, however. I had done what I had to do to assuage my conscience, I had stood in the fire, I had taken the moral high ground, I had drawn a line in the sand, I had remembered the Alamo, and all things considered, I felt that my comments had completely gotten me off the hook from the ethical perspective. That, plus the fact that I received no money for the speech, which believe you me, never, ever happens. *Like, never.*

When I think back on all the RAKs and SABs that I performed during that magical spring when my heart, like forsythia, slowly came back to life, I am particularly proud that it was in our nation's capital that I pulled off my first philanthropic hat trick. I had given my pro bono speech to the USDA in recognition of their pro-pachyrdermal policy, but had given them hell because of their craven attitude toward mice, rats, and birds. I had established a beachhead for Dolci for Dissidents, and even though I was not technically successful in finding any actual dolci, those Krispy Kremes struck me as an adequate substitute. And back at the hotel, I had again crossed paths with one of those little eco-hints that have become so prevalent in hostelries these days. Out in L.A., the Sofitel Hotel had asked me to re-use my soiled towels. The discreet little message resting on my pillow at the Red Roof Hotel in Washington concerned my sheets. It read

Together, We Can Keep It Clean

It is estimated that hotels use over 180 billion gallons of water each year. This Red Roof Inn is dedicated to helping conserve water and energy and reduce pollution caused by detergents. We invite you to participate by using just one set of bed linens during your stay.

Thank you for your participation. We will make your bed each day without changing your linens.

Let's be honest, the old Joe Queenan would have dismissed this message as a typical eco-scam enabling the tightfisted hotel chain to cut costs by having guests sleep more than one night in their smelly old sheets. But the new Joe Queenan immediately recognized the overwhelming ecological impact of this overture. So the whole time I was in Washington I slept on the bedspread, and then left a note for the maid telling her that as I hadn't even touched the sheets, it would be okay to leave them on the bed for the next guest. If everybody followed my example, there would be enough water left over to reforest the Sahara.

Think about it.

As the preceding makes clear, some of my RAKs were completely random and some were not. Dolci for Dissidents was an endeavor I planned extensively, and one that required a bit of legwork. But other senseless opportunities to perform RAKs and SABs simply fell into my lap. Take my gesture of charity to one of America's least beloved public figures.

It all started while I was going through my junk mail one morning. Because I had spent so much time writing for right-wing publications before I decided to become a good person, I was on every conservative mailing list in the country. This meant that I always had lots of kindling lying around the house waiting to be tossed into the fire. Here was a letter from the Manhattan Institute inviting me to attend a lecture by some think tank zealot who wanted to cut taxes. Right into the flames with that bad boy! Here was a communiqué from the Cato Institute asking for a handout. Straight into the fireplace! Here was an invitation to subscribe to the Moonie-owned *Washington Times*. Satan, get thee hence! And here was a letter from Bill Bennett requesting that I become a charter subscriber to a "conservative-oriented, idea-driven publishing house to bring back serious books about culture, politics, public affairs, and history to America's bookshelves!" This from an intellectual freeloader most famous for compiling an anthology of great writing by dead people who wouldn't have been caught, well, *dead* with a cultural second-story man like Bill Bennett if they were still alive. Screw you, loser.

But one night as I was poised to shred a rather voluminous letter from the Linda Tripp Legal Defense Fund, it occurred to me that my newfound antipathy toward conservative causes rested on tenuous moral underpinnings. Obviously, almost all the good things that came about in this society were the results of efforts by stupendously virtuous, left-leaning people such as Sting, Jackson, Tom of Maine, and his wife, the gifted poetess Kate of Maine. But if I was truly committed to a philosophy of practicing RAKs and SABs, wouldn't the law of averages eventually lead me to do something nice for a Republican? I mean, wasn't randomness essentially, *random*? Besides, when I read through the scriptures, I found no evidence that Jesus limited his munificence to one class or one ethnic group or one political party. Basically, He seemed to get along with just about everybody.

With this in mind, I decided that it was time to do something randomly, senselessly beautiful for Linda Tripp. Although I, like just about everyone else I knew, felt that she was a duplicitous hydra, a snake in the grass, a vile toad, she was still in a very real sense a human being. I tried to remember this as I plowed through her twelve-page pitch letter, hoping to dream up something randomly kind I could do for her. No, I was not going to send her a check to help cover her legal costs; if she hadn't taped those conversations and then been such a blabbermouth about it, she wouldn't have found herself in such a bind. But maybe there was some other way I could lend a hand. Searching for inspiration, I reread the letter. Well, as you can imagine, it was mostly boilerplate material —"I'm told you are a fair person…I stand to lose everything….They have me in their crosshairs….I feel like David up against Goliath….My children and I have our backs to the wall…." But then on page 9 I read the words, "I'm living in fear for my job and for the safety of my family and myself. The little things I always took for granted, like going to the grocery store or the gas station in privacy, seem to be gone forever."

Immediately I ran out, did what had to be done, then came back, sat down at my word processor, and wrote Ms. Tripp the following letter:

> Dear Ms. Tripp:
>
> I recently received your letter in the mail. You are correct in your assumption that I am "a fair person." And being a fair person, I do not believe for a moment that you are either a liar or a felon. This being the case, I do not think that you should be prosecuted or incarcerated for your actions. However, I do believe that secretly taping a friend's conversations is an unforgivable action—unless someone like the head of the Gambino Family was involved—so you have brought a lot of this misfortune on yourself.
>
> Being a kind and generous person, I know how difficult it must be for you to shop for groceries in privacy. With this in mind, I have done some grocery shopping for you. Please find enclosed a box of Health Valley organic blueberry tarts, a package of Newman's Own organic pretzels, a box of Kavli crispbread, a bag of St. John's wort tortilla chips, a container of Chai decaffeinated organic tea, a package of St. John's wort tea, and some organic Cajun jerky. I know I have loaded up on the St. John's wort products, but the tone of your letter made it sound like you were a little bit down. St. John's wort is an ancient natural remedy that is thought to be very effective in the treatment of depression.

By the way, do you like coffee? If you do, please let me know, and I will call the folks at Kalani Organica and get them to send you some shade-grown coffee. I don't know if shade-grown coffee actually existed when your legal travails began, but purchasing this ecologically nurturing beverage prevents bird habitats from being destroyed and also vastly reduces pollution of our rivers, and I think everybody should try it. So let me know. Or, if you prefer organic tea, I can have some of it shipped out.

Best of luck in all your endeavors,

Joe Queenan

P.S. I am also sending along some cents-off coupons from Tom's of Maine. Be well.

Then I sidled down the street and shipped this organic care package off in the mail. I rewarded myself for performing the most random RAK of my entire life by eating an entire pint of Ben & Jerry's ice cream, which I got for free by cashing in one of the coupons that my socially conscious long-distance telephone company sent me every month. Yes, I felt pretty good about myself, pretty up, pretty up, pretty *up, up and away*, as the righteous babe Ani DiFranco might have put it. The only thing missing? I really wished that Ben & Jerry's had a St. John's wort flavor, so I could have sent some of that, freeze-dried, to Linda Tripp, as well. But you can't have everything.

9 • Reach Out and

Touch Somebody

I would be lying if I said that everything I did during my spiritual makeover was equally pleasurable. No matter how much I admired Robin Williams's charitable work in projects such as *Comic Relief*, it didn't make watching movies like *Patch Adams* any more enjoyable. The hemp soap from the Body Shop made me smell like I'd spent three nights on a bender in the rain forest. And I was spending so much time being generous with my soy-based, recyclable La Leche League Message!Checks that I wished there was an umbrella group called Overnight Virtue to whom I could write a single check once a year, authorizing them to redistribute the money, using some kind of moral means test, to the whales, the Spirit Bear, the Dalai Lama, or some other deserving cause, mammal, persecutee.

Finally, no matter how I tried, I found it impossible to fantasize about women in organic or alternative underwear because natural fibers are inherently non-salacious. Though I did see an ad in some organic publication for a firm called Alternative Undies (www.PantyParlour.com) offering bikini panties, hip huggers, thongs, tap pants, and even chemises in a number of organic materials (cotton, angora, hemp, and silk), I was incapable of getting excited about women in any of these fibers. Even Kim Basinger. But particularly Anita Roddick. Sometimes I would find myself daydreaming about a totally natural-fiber world where even the dominatrixes had to wear organic corsets and garter belts made of hemp. It didn't sound like much fun.

Because of my Jewel of the Schuylkill, blue-collar, eggs-and-scrapple eating habits, dining on deeply organic food never became second nature to me. This is something I found out the hard way. Around seven o'clock on April 22, 1999, I suddenly realized that Earth Day was almost over and I hadn't done anything like visit a bird sanctuary or apprise my children of the dangers posed to the environment by emissions of methane gas from cows. I think I can be forgiven for this absentmind-edness, because Earth Day isn't that big a deal any more and because I live in the suburbs where it's pretty much Earth Day every day of the week. Like, we separate glass and stuff.

Still, I felt bad. Letting Earth Day go by without notice was like missing Christmas or Thanksgiving or Independence Day or Cinco de Mayo. So I immediately rushed into the city and hustled down to Black-Eyed Suzie's Organic Café, an award-winning restaurant in the heart of Manhattan's East Village. I chose Black-Eyed Suzie's because it had been rated the number-one organic restaurant by *New York Naturally*, a sort of macrobiotic *Zagat Survey*. Although I had eaten vegetarian lasagna and free-range chicken before, this was the very first time I had dined in an explicitly organic restaurant, because until recently I had been a malignant carnivore who thought this kind of stuff was a big joke. Anyway, to make a long story short, after perusing the special Earth Day menu, I ordered the coconut Thai vegetables with tofu, which was bland but edible, but I also ordered the Immune System Builder (an amalgam of celery, carrot, apple, beet, parsley, and wheatgrass juices), and that made me sick. Or, put it this way, the drink itself might not have made me sick, but when I foolishly decided to wash it down with a buckwheat chaser, well, the rest of the evening was Upchuck Canyon.

There's a valuable lesson to be learned here: Don't try to get it all back at once. If you've been a fast-food, Coke-swilling junkie all your life, you can't turn things around overnight with wheatgrass sundaes and kale-based shakes any more than a person who's spent his life reading Tom Clancy can suddenly switch to Thomas Mann. Looking back on things, I'm sure that if I'd played it close to the vest with a Chai Smoothie or a blue-green algae cocktail, things would have been fine. But no, Mr. Big Spender had to go for the brass ring with the wheatgrass aperitif. And pay the price he did.

While we're on the subject of organic dining, this is probably a good place to discuss alternative living modalities in general. One of the questions people often ask recovering vile people is how far into the world of organic homeopathic empyrean rebirthing you have to penetrate in order to change your personality. For example, is it necessary to participate in Vision Quests? Attend seasonal cleansing classes? Master neuro-linguistic programming or Ericksonian hypnosis? Is homeopathy an indispensable component of being a good person? Rolfing? Cranisacral therapy? Is it essential that one sign up for a Reiki healing circle? Where do lymphatic drainage and colonic irrigation fit into the overall picture? Or, for that matter, Healing Breath and applied iridology? Finally, and perhaps most important, will it make you a more complete human being—and therefore a better person—if you sign up for courses in Ayurvedic stress management techniques? Or should you stick with more strait-laced Hakomic therapy and holographic repatterning?

Basically, my philosophy in this area is to go with the flow, accept the fact that different strokes are appropriate for different folks, and try and catch the wind. But the one thing a stranger in the strange land of virtue must take steps to ensure is that the new components of his lifestyle are culturally, ethnically, and psychologically contiguous with the psychic substratum of the abiding, non-mutative elements that comprise the pan-galactic grappa of his personality. For example, I have never seriously investigated Ayurvedic stress management approaches or Paramhansa Yoganandan self-realization techniques because I am Irish-American and grew up in a working-class environment in an obsessively proletarian city and am not culturally predisposed toward anything from the Mysterious East that would make me look like an idiot or get my ass kicked when I go to Flyers games.

I am not saying that people who practice Ayurvedic stress management approaches or Paramhansa Yoganandan self-realization techniques are themselves foolish, or that Ayurvedic stress management approaches and Paramhansa Yoganandan self-realization techniques are in fact foolish themselves, but merely that in the type of neighborhood my family lives in—and indeed, the types of neighborhoods most people's families live in—a person announcing that he was now practicing Ayurvedic stress management approaches or Paramhansa Yoganandan self-realization techniques would automatically be dismissed as a granola-head and, very possibly, a full-fledged jerk-off. I am sorry, but that is the way it is.

Disinclination to be perceived as a buffoon aside, I had another reason for shunning the more extravagant precincts of the Holistically Homeopathic Hemisphere. In no way, shape, or form did I want my program of emotional self-refurbishing to end up making me look like a spiritual carpetbagger, a dabbler, a will-o'-the-wisp, a dilettante. In virtue, as in vice, I favored an aggressive, visceral lifestyle and was inimical to anything that was passive, introspective, or encouraged a retreat from the real world. In saying this, I am not passing judgment on the world of Holistic Homeopathia; I am only saying that in such a milieu I would feel no more comfortable than Mumia Abu-Jumal would feel at a Fraternal Order of Police convention. Conventional vegetarianism was the only concession I was prepared to make to the world of Ayurvedic Neuro-linguistic Reikian Yoga. Feldenkrais aficionados were going to have to make do without me.

It will come as no shock to the reader that I did not take to goodness as a duck takes to water. It was one thing to write a check and adopt a wolf or a Spirit Bear, quite another to be nice to other human beings who may or not have deserved such amity. Thus, over the course of my enterprise, I had many false starts. Initially, I decided to start being a better person on my birthday, November 3, but then I got an assignment to make fun of Rod Stewart, so I had to delay a month. Next I decided to start being good on Thanksgiving, but then I got an assignment to make fun of Fergie. After that it was Christmas, and New Year's, and then the Feast of the Epiphany, and Lincoln's Birthday, but the assignments to make fun of people kept pouring in. In fact, I did not get around to becoming a full-fledged good person, making an honest effort to be virtuous twenty-four hours a day, until late February 1999. That's when I stopped taking any writing assignments that involved being mean to other human beings, and devoted all my energies to improving the human condition.

How did I spend my time? Well, here was a typical day:

6:00 A.M. Hearty breakfast of shade-grown coffee purchased from Kalani Organica. Bowl of organic granola topped with Edensoy juice.

6:20 A.M. Order humane deer repellent online from Greatergood.com, knowing that five percent of the purchase price ($18) will go to benefit Mothers Against Violence in America. Also make mental note to order some Colorado Potato Beetle Bacterium and Predatory Midges later in the year as a Christmas gift for my wife, an avid gardener.

7:30 A.M. Walk to office and vote for the new Amnesty International board of directors. There are nine candidates, and each AI member gets to cast six votes; I don't know very much about anyone's credentials, so I decide to cast my votes for the five women and one minority, figuring I can't go far wrong by following such a manifestly politically correct policy.

7:45 A.M.. Send my son's tooth to the Radiation and Public Health Project to determine the level of nuclear radiation in children's teeth.

8:00 A.M. Listen to a few tracks off the new Ani DiFranco album *Up. Up. Up*, which was manufactured by damaged people employed by the Righteous Babe in her abjectly nonglamorous hometown of Buffalo, New York.

8:15 A.M. Adopt a wolf from Defenders of Wildlife.

8:30 A.M. Send a check to Steve Allen's Parents Television Council to protest the vermin in Hollywood who are leading our children right down a moral sewer.

8:45 A.M. Throw out two bottles of shampoo because the disgusting manufacturers experiment on lab animals.

9:00 A.M. Write a letter to Roger Enricho, president and CEO of Pepsico, telling him that unless his company stops advertising its products on billboards at bullfighting arenas in Spain, I will no longer buy Doritos or Tropicana orange juice. Since I love Doritos and Tropicana orange juice, this is a big step. Giving up Pepsi would be no big deal, as I hate soft drinks.

9:15 A.M. Join the Natural Resources Defense Council.

9:30 A.M. Send a few bucks to the Guide Dog Foundation for the Blind.

10:00 A.M. Spend three hours reading my phone bill from Working Assets. Of the six pages, only one is taken up by my calls; the other five are devoted to a bevy of social injustices and ecological crimes. I am asked to contact the chief executive office of Kodak and tell him to shut down the company's hazardous waste incinerators until they are equipped with state-of-the-art pollution controls. I do. I am asked to enroll in the New York AutoCitizenLetter Program, which will automatically send an angry letter to a targeted New York leader each month for just $1.80. I do. (This program is not to be confused with the National AutoCitizenLetter, which also costs $1.80 a pop.) I am informed that my phone calls are helping to eliminate the *trokosi* tradition in Ghana, whereby young girls are turned over to the local shrines "to atone for a crime which has been committed in the family." I am relieved. I am also provided with a socially conscious reading list, including Germaine Greer's new book *The Whole Woman*, and am told how to order these books directly from Working Assets. I'll think about it. I am also given President Clinton's phone number, so I can call him and tell him to stop the bombing in Kosovo, but because I doubt that I will get through, I instead authorize Working Assets to send him an AutoCitizenLetter. While I'm at it, I also check the box instructing my phone company to send Speaker of the House Dennis Hastert an AutoCitizenLetter urging him to schedule a vote on the bipartisan Shays-Meehan bill, which will clean up the campaign finance mess.

1:00 P.M. Lunch of organic tofu wieners and strawberry kefir.

1:30 P.M. Sign and mail a petition to be filed with the American Anti-Vivisection Society's scientific affiliate, the Alternatives Research & Development Foundation, protesting the United States Department of Agriculture's half-assed, insensitive regulation of mice, rats, and birds under the Animal Welfare Act.

1:45 P.M. Duck a call from my dear old friend Kathy Rich, because she is an editor at *Allure,* a magazine despised by the anti-fur movement.

2:00 P.M. Write a letter to the queen of Spain telling her that unless she acts to stop the abuse of greyhounds in her country's racetracks, I will stop eating paella and tell all my friends to avoid Picasso exhibitions.

2:15 P.M. Turn down an opportunity to be on Judith Regan's weekend talk show because Judith Regan is not a very nice person and would have wanted me to say mean things about nice people.

2:30 P.M. Send a few bucks to the Center for Marine Conservation.

2:45 P.M. Turn down a proposal from *GQ* to write a cruel story.

3:00 P.M. Send a few bucks to Farm Sanctuary, an organization that defends "downed" animals. I do not actually know what downed animals are, but it sounds like they need help.

3:30 P.M. Send a few bucks to the Nature Conservancy.

3:50 P.M. Write a letter to the chairman and president of a major tire manufacturer letting him know that if he does not do something about his company's toxic emissions, he can just forget about me ever buying another tire from his shameful outfit.

4:25 P.M. Write an angry letter to Tom Clark, president of Nike, protesting the TV commercial where a football player dresses a chicken in a jersey, chases her, and then cooks her, because "the abuse of animals—well, fowl—can soon lead to the abuse of humans, and then before you know it—Boom! Kosovo!"

4:45 P.M. Order two more pounds of shade-grown coffee from Kalani Organic of Seattle, Washington.

5:30 P.M. Head into the city, listening to Peter Gabriel's *Greatest Hits* on my DiscMan.

6:00 P.M. Stick some of those surplus bumper stickers that my wife so emphatically rejected on people's cars. Originally, I thought it would be fun to subvert the dominant paradigm by affixing a sticker reading IF YOU CAN'T TRUST ME WITH A CHOICE, HOW CAN YOU TRUST ME WITH A CHILD? to a vehicle sporting pro-life messagery. But now I decide that this would simply be mean. So, as soon as I find a pro-choice automobile, I add one of my own pro-choice slogans to the socially conscious bumper. The stickers reading FRIENDS DON'T LET FRIENDS VOTE REPUBLICAN I affix to an apolitical telephone pole.

7:00 P.M. Join a friend for dinner at a Tibetan restaurant, obliquely lending solidarity to the Dalai Lama.

8:30 P.M. Pick up some body bars and other animal-abuse–free products at the Body Shop.

9:00 P.M. Practice frugal philanthropy for a couple of hours, distributing small gifts of cash to bag people, street musicians, the generally needy.

11:00 P.M. Head home, listening to Sting's "They Dance Alone," which deals with the *desaparecidos* of Chile (or maybe it was Argentina), while reading *Mother Jones* and the *Utne Reader.*

12:00 A.M. Begin sleeping the sleep of the just.

When I say that this particular evening, like so many others, was devoted to the practice of frugal philanthropy, I should perhaps be a bit clearer about what I mean. Frugal philanthropy has a number of vital psychological components, most notably that the philanthropist experiences more of a rush from his generosity if he actually gets to interact with the person whose life he is immeasurably improving than if he simply sends a check to the Children's Aid Society.

For example, one day I read an article in the *New York Times* about Paul Newman's philanthropic experiences. The article said that when a third-grade kid from Wilmington, Delaware, wrote a letter asking Newman to sponsor him in a reading marathon to benefit people with multiple sclerosis, the actor wrote a check for $500. Conversely, when a fifty-year-old woman living with her mother asked for $120,000 so that she could buy a house and put some distance between her and her mother, the actor turned her down.

Here is one of the many areas where Newman and I have a profound philosophical disagreement. If I received two letters like these, and I had $100 million to give away, I might very well write a check to the little kid in the reading marathon. But I would only write a check for $100. The other $400 I would send to the woman who wanted to get away from her mother, because even though it would not be enough to buy her a house, it would be enough to cover a couple of weeks in the local EconoLodge, where she could take a breather from Mom and hopefully get her act together. Four hundred dollars would also be enough to get a bus out of town and start a new life elsewhere. The kind of philanthropy practiced by Paul Newman is helpful but obvious, since people with MS or AIDS or reading problems obviously take precedence over people who can't stand their mothers. The type of phil-anthropy to which I had committed myself (Dolci for Dissidents, care packages for Linda Tripp, the Krishnaswamy Kaper) came directly out of left field; because these RAKs and SABs had such an unexpected, illogical quality it enabled my largessees to revel in the miraculous, per-suaded as they were that a complete stranger might show up out of nowhere one day and give them enough money to completely change their lives. Or at least stay in the EconoLodge for a week. Here, my greatest influence was not Paul Newman or Ben & Jerry but the superb 1950s TV program *The Millionaire*. The only difference: I was working with smaller numbers.

The type of philanthropy I strove to practice was similar to that of the Boston man who would call up six "unsung heroes" each year and inform them that they had just won $20,000. These people would then apprise their friends of their good fortune, and little by little word would spread throughout the community that mankind was not cast adrift in a cruel, insensitive universe, that a sudden inflow of cash could surge through the transom any day of the week if you only believed in miracles. And, as Alice Munro once said, people who believe in miracles are never surprised when they happen.

What I had in mind was not the performance or subsidization of miracles, because I did not have the cash to bankroll anything on such an epic scale. No, what I was increasingly committing myself to can be summed up in a single phrase as *extremely random but very inexpensive acts of kindness and equally economical, albeit senseless, acts of beauty*. In other words, X-treme RAKs and SABs. Let me give an example. In 1998, the gifted writer Vince Passaro published an article in *Harper's* magazine complaining about how hard it was to raise his family of four on $99,651 a year. (In fact, at the time the article appeared, the Passaro family was $63,000 in debt.) Predictably, everybody in creation jumped all over him, filling the magazine's mailbags with jeremiads about what a horrible, insensitive person he was. But Passaro had said nothing less than the truth: It *is* impossible to raise a family of four in Manhattan on $99,651, and I for one admired his courage in admitting it. Now, tired of all the abuse he'd been forced to endure, I dropped him a note.

> Dear Mr. Passaro,
>
> I read that story you wrote last year about not being able to make ends meet even though you and your wife earn something like $99,000 a year. Then I read all the angry letters from the usual outraged Jacobins. Personally, I know exactly how hard it must be to raise a family in New York on that kind of money; that's why I don't live in New York and you wouldn't catch me dead writing for *Harper's*, even though it is assuredly one of the finest magazines in the country. In any case, I recently decided to turn over a new leaf by practicing senseless acts of random beauty, but am getting tired of sending my money to protect imperiled Spirit Bears and downed cows. So enclosed please find a check for $50 from one of my many new foundations, *The Make a Wish, As Long As the Wish Doesn't Cost More Than Fifty Bucks, Foundation*. Use it to take your wife to lunch or something. Meanwhile, keep up the fine work. You are a very gifted writer, and that skinflint Lapham should give you a raise.
>
> Sincerely,
> Joe Queenan

Another fine example of economy-class kindness was my experience with the *Ave Maria* guy. The Ave Maria guy was an Oriental street musician I used to bump into just about every time I rode the subway in Manhattan. Unlike most street musicians, who would drive everyone crazy with their unbearable renditions of "The Sounds of Silence" and "The Cat's in the Cradle," the Ave Maria guy always sang Franz

Schubert's glorious hymn "Ave Maria," and he always sang it beautiful-
ly. As far as I know, it was the only piece he ever performed. And I used
to love hearing him perform it.

But eventually I noticed a minor hitch in his delivery. He wasn't
putting the song over quite right. At first I thought I might have imagined this, but the next time I heard him and in numerous subsequent
hearings, he committed the same errors. Chatting with fellow
cognoscenti on the platform, I confirmed that the man, for whatever
the reason, was habitually mis-singing the hymn. So one night I stopped
off at my local record store, made a few purchases, then rushed home
and wrote him this letter:

> Dear Sir:
> Several months ago, I first heard you perform Franz
> Schubert's classic "Ave Maria" on a subway platform in New
> York. I was very impressed, as were many of the other com-
> muters and tourists on the train platform. As you well know,
> from a musical standpoint, the subway has become a chamber of
> horrors, with incompetent but earnest neo-folkies caterwauling
> such abominations as "Helpless, Helpless," "Blowin' in the
> Wind," and "The Sounds of Silence" on train platforms all over
> the metropolitan area. Things have gotten so bad that I have
> deliberately altered my commuting patterns, striving to avoid
> subway stations where I know from bitter experience that I will
> be forced to listen to blood-curdling renditions of Billy Joel and
> Peter, Paul & Mary songs. Not that the originals were that much
> better.
>
> I do have one reservation, however. About halfway through
> the first verse of "Ave Maria," I notice that you have a tendency
> to cheat on one of the difficult parts, sending your voice down a
> register when it should actually go up. At first I thought this was
> because you had a cold, but I have heard you perform the song
> at least a dozen times now, and every single time, you sing the
> difficult passage incorrectly. Frankly, I find this a bit annoying.
>
> Were this purely a matter of personal taste, I would hesi-

tate to bring it to your attention. But a number of impromptu
conversations I have had with other sophisticated commuters
confirms that they also find your unorthodox, nay incorrect, rendition a tad disorienting. Since you are already so close to perfection, bringing a bright and unexpected ray of sunlight into the
dank world of the Manhattan commuter—a phenomenon the
French describe as *insolite*, a term that has no equivalent in our
graceless, guttural idiom—why not do things right?

Not for one second do I think you have been mis-singing
the hymn just to bust our collective subterranean chops, or out
of some idiosyncratic need to provide your own eccentric interpretation of the Schubert classic. No, it is now my conviction
that you simply never learned how to sing the song properly.
Accordingly, I have purchased a compact disc entitled *Ave Maria*,
which contains 15 different renditions of the various "Ave
Marias," including five versions of the Schubert composition.
From a careful listening to these performances, I am certain that
you can expeditiously nail down the correct version of the wonderful hymn and raise yourself to new levels of artistic excellence. This will almost certainly lead to more and larger donations from a grateful public. Though, obviously, I cannot guaran-
tee this.

I trust that you will accept this gift in the spirit of bounty
and bonhomie in which it is offered. Your artistry, virtually
unparalleled in the New York Metropolitan Transportation
System, has already brought me much happiness over the dark
winter months. I anxiously look forward to hearing your new
and improved version of "Ave Maria." You are a bright beacon of
sophistication in a sea of primeval detritus, and I wish you all the
best.

Joe Queenan
A Fellow Schubertophile

P.S. "Für Elise" is another delightful bagatelle you might
look into. Very popular among street performers on the Isle de

la Cité in Paris. But I would give the Pachelbel *Canon* a wide
berth. Charming on first hearing, but after a while it begins to
smack of Renaissance Teshianism.

I thought it was a pretty nice letter—succinct, respectful—so I
sealed the package containing the CD and letter and stuck it in my bag.
The next time I went into the city, I would make sure to give it to the
Ave Maria guy.

Alas, as had been the case with Dolci for Dissidents, things did not
come off like clockwork. The next time I went into the city, the Ave
Maria Guy was nowhere to be seen. Ditto my next visit. As a matter of
fact, from the time I bought the CD and wrote the letter, I never saw
him on my regular subway platforms again.

Eventually, my mission became an obsession. I spent hours haunt-
ing the subway system, buttonholing other street musicians: "There's
five bucks in it if you can help me find the Ave Maria guy." But no one
knew where he was. Few had ever laid eyes on the guy, though one or
two knew his lore. Finally, I became so obsessed with running my quar-
ry to earth that I spent three entire days wandering from subway station
to subway station. Though I recalled that I had usually seen him either
at the downtown Lexington Avenue platform at Grand Central Station
or at the uptown express Lexington Avenue platform at 59th and
Lexington, I did not limit my search to those venues. I tried the busy
Times Square station at nine in the morning. As usual, the fine jazz trio
was there playing their tasty licks, as were the industrious Peruvian
drummers and pennywhistlers and a hefty African-American woman
belting out an appealing congeries of Motownian chestnuts. But no Ave
Maria guy.

At Union Square, I crossed paths with several saxophonists and
folk singers, one of whom I paid $20 to stop playing "The Piano Man"
—especially since he was playing it on the guitar—but no Ave Maria
Guy. Nor was the Ave Maria guy to be found at the West 4th Street
Station in Greenwich Village or under Penn Station at 32nd and 7th.
Finally, on the third day, I sidled up to a very talented young jazz pianist
in the bowels of the seedy Port Authority station and asked for guid-

ance. I wondered out loud if the assorted street musicians simply divvied up all the subway platforms each week, if somewhere in the bowels of the system there was not some bureaucrat sticking little pins in a map reading

> 59th St. Uptown No. 1 platform: Jimi Hendrix impersonator, 9–6.

> 14th St. Downtown No. 6 platform: Stan Getz soundalike, 7–12.

> 5th Avenue Downtown R and N platform: Cat Stevens guy, 9–5.

> Penn Station, Uptown A Platform: Ave Maria guy, 12–8.

But he assured me that this was not the case, that locations were decided on a first-come, first-served basis. And he had never seen or heard of the Ave Maria Guy.

Undeterred, I continued my fruitless search, wandering out to Jackson Heights in Queens and Borough Hall in Brooklyn Heights, theorizing that the man's mildly annoying renditions of "Ave Maria" had so worn on the nerves of commuters that he had been banished to the outer boroughs, where a less sophisticated, more working-class ridership might be mesmerized by his craft. Alas, he was nowhere to be found.

To this day I still curse myself for not getting to him in time. Once, a friendly *saxo romantico* player on the No. 4 and 5 downtown line at 59th and Lexington told me that the Ave Maria guy usually worked the other end of the platform. I spent the next month checking out that venue every time I was in the neighborhood, but he never surfaced. Had I been successful in passing along the CD, he would have learned how to sing the gorgeous hymn properly, and might still be flourishing in the inner sanctum of the New York subway system. Instead, I fear, he has gone into another line of work or perhaps been cast out into the darkness. In the end, I was so dismayed by my failure that I had to brew myself a cup of St. John's wort tea, a beverage in the Ayurvedic tradition which has been used for over two thousand years for the treatment of depression.

Whenever I hit a roadblock such as this, I would immediately commit myself to another, quite different RAK or SAB. Sometimes, this merely involved getting the old noggin going and dreaming up ways I could help other people who practiced RAKs to either practice more of them or to raise the bar a little. That's what inspired me to send the following letter to Tom Chappell, founder of Tom's of Maine:

> Dear Tom:
> A couple of years ago, you gave a talk at the Old Dutch Reformed Church in Tarrytown, New York, during which you spoke of the special mission of your company. Although the talk was well received, many of the people in attendance were secretly grossed out when you started talking about lab animals, as senior citizens generally do not like to talk about such topics, and by and large could care less about the plight of guinea pigs, hamsters, and most especially rats, because they already have their own problems.
>
> I, however, was very impressed by your talk, so much so that I stopped using Crest. Indeed, after reading the materials printed on the side of your dental products, I have become very interested in the Anti-Vivisection Movement. I have sent away for the shopping guide from the Anti-Vivisection Society, and now refuse to patronize companies that experiment on animals. I thank you for providing the website of that organization on your toothpaste literature.
>
> I am writing today because I was wondering whether you have any plans to put the pictures of laboratory animals on the sides of your products. You probably remember that when the pictures of kidnapped kids started turning up on the sides of milk containers, kidnappings dropped off enormously, in part because even kidnappers began to realize that kids were cute. I

wonder if the same thing might not happen with guinea pigs and rats. Perhaps if you put photos of cuddly little hamsters and rats on the side of your toothpaste, the public would stop thinking of them as disgusting predators and would thus care more about their tragic predicament. Then, every night, when people were brushing their teeth they could think how lucky they were not to be trapped in some laboratory somewhere getting all carved up.

I throw out this suggestion for whatever it is worth. And yes, I know you would have to find the right animals, and the right photographer, and be careful with the lighting. In the meantime, I was wondering if you could send me a copy of your latest annual report as I wish to learn more about your unique approach to management. I was also wondering if there is anywhere I can buy copies of your wife's poetry, as I have heard it is quite enthralling.

Good luck, Tom! It is people like you like you who make this country great. Keep practicing random acts of senseless kindness and senseless acts of random beauty, and so on, as nobody does it better!

Best wishes,

Joe Queenan

Several weeks later, I received a personal letter from Patti Murphy, who identified herself as the "Consumer Dialogue Team Leader" at Tom's of Maine. Patti told me that Tom had personally read my letter, but had not had the time to respond to it, so he had forwarded it to her. Patti assured me that my suggestions about putting rats on the company's toothpaste packages were much appreciated, and said that she had "passed them along to our Brand Team for their review." She also told me that Kate's poetry had been published in magazines such as *Chrysalis*, but that she did not "yet" have a book out. Patti also said that she was sending along a copy of *The Tom's Times*, a periodical filled to overflowing with articles about productive renewal of purpose, holistic stewardship, hearts guided by "the mission," and oral hygiene. Finally, she was sending along a bunch of cents-off coupons.

To a frugal philanthropist, these were the kinds of responses that made it all worthwhile. So even though I didn't need any, I ran out and bought some more Tom's of Maine toothpaste (using my cents-off coupon, of course), exchanged my Working Assets coupon for a free pint of Ben & Jerry's Rainforest Crunch, then raced back home, gobbled up the dessert in one sitting, and clambered upstairs to brush my teeth. What a treat it was to question this much reality, challenge this much authority, and subvert this many dominant paradigms all in one day! I couldn't wait till tomorrow.

10. Sorry Seems

to Be the Hardest Word

One day, while going through my personal files, I happened upon a folder filled with angry letters I had received over the years. From the time I had become a journalist, I had squirreled away the most personal hate mail that had been sent to me, figuring that I would one day make a pilgrimage across America, visiting all the people who had expressed displeasure with my work—particularly those who had threatened to punch my lights out—and then repackage my experiences into a road book. What did I do with the letters from people who admired my work? I threw them out. Both of them.

Now I understood that this was a terribly cynical way to go through life. On careful review of the situation, I realized that I had sinned against humanity on two counts. Morally, I had transgressed the natural law by trying to reap economic benefit from the pain I had inflicted on my reading public. Professionally, I had sullied my escutcheon by failing to respond in a timely fashion to readers who had taken the time to write to me. Now I aimed to correct that situation. I bought a big roll of stamps, addressed a huge stack of envelopes, sat down in front of my computer, and got cracking.

The first letter went out to a New Hampshire woman who had written to *Forbes* to complain about an article I had written poking fun at New Age guides to personal finance. Here is what I wrote in response:

> Dear Pamela,
>
> Almost 10 years ago you wrote *Forbes* the enclosed letter complaining about a story in which I made fun of people who "eat too much brown rice." Your criticism was right on target. As you point out, brown rice does provide both high fiber and important vitamins and minerals. What's more, I knew this at the time I wrote my story, as my wife is a bit of a "brown rice nut," and we have been eating it for years. I admit it: It was a cheap shot. I merely resorted to this gambit because "brown rice," like "Birkenstocks" and "granola," are shorthand terms that immediately conjure up images of New Age airheadedness in the minds of *Forbes'* hard-boiled, right-wing, white-rice-eating readership. I apologize for saying it, and I also apologize for how long it has taken me to write this letter. Much of my time in the past 10 years has been devoted to becoming mildly famous (ever seen my weekly "Average Joe" column in *TV Guide* or caught my numerous appearances on *Politically Incorrect*?). But the real reason it has taken me so long to respond is because I have always been a fundamentally horrible person, and only recently have taken steps to correct this moral infirmity. In any case, sorry about the brown rice wisecrack, and enclosed please find a few bucks to go out and buy yourself a fresh supply.
>
> *Bon appetit!*
>
> Joe Queenan

As was my wont, I slipped three bucks into the envelope, because I honestly believe that the personal touch works best, and nothing says it like hard cash.

The next person I contacted was a man from Hoover, Alabama, who had written me a letter a few months earlier. In it he said that he had just finished reading my book *Red Lobster, White Trash, and The Blue Lagoon*, and didn't much care for it. Since I had once written a story for *GQ* about giving refunds to people who had shelled out their hard-earned money to watch dumb movies, he was anxious to know whether I would give a refund to someone unfortunate enough to have purchased and read my dumb book. Specifically, him.

Although I was not entirely happy with the tone of this letter, I decided to write back to him anyway. Here is the dispatch in question:

> Dear Tom:
>
> I received your letter of February 6, 1999, requesting a refund for your purchase of *Red Lobster, White Trash, and The Blue Lagoon*, which you referred to as "stupid." I am more than happy to refund your money as I do not want to bring any more unhappiness into the world, but I have not been able to contact you though I have called your house at least 10 times in the past month. If you do, in fact, want a refund, please tell me exactly how much you paid for the book, including tax. And yes, I will be requiring proof of purchase (Visa bill, register receipt, whatever) as I do not want to fall for the old "I Hated Your Book And Would Like a Refund Even Though I Never Actually Bought It Scam." So please send me the relevant information and I will cut you a check posthaste.
>
> I must point out that this is a one-of-a-kind offer that will not be repeated. Currently, my collection of irreverent essays *If You're Talking to Me, Your Career Must Be in Trouble* is available in paperback, and next February I have two new books coming out. But if you purchase these books and are disappointed by them, I will not refund your money, as they will be just as "stupid" as my last book and it will be your own fault for buying them. *Caveat emptor*, Tom!
>
> Best wishes,
>
> Joe Queenan

P.S. Here's a buck to get you started.

About three weeks later, Tom sent me a second letter, enclosed in a package containing my book. This time he told me to keep my money, because he could not in conscience ask for a refund from "a gentleman" who would take the time and energy to respond to such a "juvenile and insulting letter."

Inside, he had enclosed the $1 bill I had sent in my earlier letter.

This missive distressed me more than the previous one. Because he had spent $2.75 to ship my book back, Tom was now out the cost of the book, the $2.75 postage, the 33 cents for the original stamp, plus any other incidental costs (parking, sundries). Frankly, I was baffled by this missive. The use of the term "gentleman" suggested that we were getting into one of these neo-antebellum crinoline-and-magnolia, you-be-Rhett, I'll-be-Ravenall situations that could eventually lead to flintlocks at twenty paces. At first, Tom was the injured party because he had purchased a book that he ended up disliking. Then I became the injured party because he said my book was so bad that I should give him a refund. Now Tom had the upper hand again because he was gallantly forgoing both the cost of the book and the proffered refund. This in spite of the overall tone of my letter, which, I now had to admit, was suffused with a haughty, condescending quality. Stymied, I tried to think what Saint Francis of Assisi or Sting would have done in a situation like this, and I finally decided to send the following letter:

Dear Tom,

I have just received your letter, the book, and the dollar bill, and thank you kindly. But rest assured, not for one moment did I view your request as "juvenile" or "insulting." Actually, I thought it was quite clever. By and large, I welcome the good-natured give-and-take between authors and the public, and frankly feel that your demand for a refund was a good-natured way of taking the mickey out of Mr. Big Shot.

While I am flattered by your description of me as a "gentleman," I feel that your gracious decision to forgo your refund provides mute testimony that you yourself are not entirely devoid of gentlemanly virtues. As George Orwell once put it in

A Spanish Testament, "Somos caballeros." It is in this spirit of affection and respect that I request that you accept my offer of a complete refund for the book, as well as full reimbursement for the shipping costs. It is one of the deep ironies of my career that I have rarely been as touched by a gesture from a well-wisher as I have been by your gesture of disapprobation. I wish you well.

    Yours Truly,

    I Remain

    Joe Queenan

    Fellow Gentleman

One day while reading a story about forgiveness in the *Utne Reader,* I realized that there was a gaping hole in my edifice of moral self-rectification. Up until now I had been smoothing over ruffled feathers with ordinary people who were neither rich nor powerful—salt-of-the-earth types who lived by the sweat of their brow and the skin of their teeth, whose nose was perpetually to the grindstone, whose shoulder was always to the wheel.

Big deal. Anybody could "sort of" apologize in relative secrecy to people who were probably leading grim lives of quiet desperation out in the hinterland where the rubber met the road less traveled. But what about people with more of a public profile, people with a little more cachet? Were they not equally worthy of an apology? And not a half-hearted apology, but a 24-karat one? Yes, I decided, they were. And though it cut me to the quick to get down in the dirt and grovel, I saw little choice in the matter. So I rolled up my sleeves and began writing penitent letters to all kinds of angry readers, and not just harmless schlubs. I apologized to authors whose books I had lambasted. I apologized to civic leaders whose hometowns I had mocked. I apologized to corporate leaders who had taken offense at my characterization of their management styles, advertising campaigns, or products. In fact, I sometimes wrote apology letters to people not so much because I felt that I had been especially unfair to them but because it struck me that a personal apology from a hard-boiled son of a bitch like me might convince them that the world was a better place to live and that man *qua* man was not incapable of redemption.

For example, back in 1995 I had written an article in *Chief Executive* magazine ridiculing the concept of "Casual Fridays," contending that when employees were allowed to wear frivolous or even silly fabrics such as flannel, they were more likely to behave in a frivolous and silly fashion and pay much less attention to their work. Specifically, I said that I would never place my money with a brokerage firm that allowed its employees to dress casually on Friday or any other day. A few months later, *Chief Executive* forwarded me an angry letter from a clothing manufacturer based in Louisville, Kentucky.

In it, Allan H. Fine, co-president of M. Fine & Sons Manufacturing Co., identified his company as "one of the foremost manufacturers and marketers of flannel shirts and denim jeans in the United States." As such, he was livid that I would dare to describe flannel as a silly fabric. Quite to the contrary, Fine protested, his flannel products were "100% cotton" and "of high quality," as well as being "warm," "durable," and "comfortable."

Basically, Fine felt I had erred by foolishly equating "goofing off" with comfort, and said it was "a sad state of affairs" when Americans were no longer "broadminded enough" to believe that a comfortably clad employee was still capable of doing an honest day's work. In his opinion, what this country needed was not just a Casual Friday but a "casual everyday." Now, that'd be one Fine day!

For more than three years, that letter had been gathering dust in my files, waiting to be incorporated into some sneering article about zany hate mail. Now, I had an entirely different idea of what to do with it. Frankly, it was about time I got off my high horse and answered it. Here's what I wrote:

> Dear Mr. Fine:
> Three years ago, you sent the enclosed letter to *Chief Executive* magazine. For a number of reasons, mostly related to my own avarice, I have not until now taken the time to respond. I regret the delay, but assure you that I have given your comments considerable thought and greatly value your input.
> Your points about comfort are well taken. However, comfort can be achieved via a number of non-flannel fabrics that do not require loss of *gravitas*. And *gravitas* is an important issue. Let me point out, for example, that the principal reason Lamar

Alexander's 1996 presidential campaign ended so dismally was because his decision to run for the highest office in the land while wearing flannel shirts made him appear to be somewhat… dare I say it…silly in the eyes of the general public. A general public, might I add, that included many, many flannel-wearing voters.

In conclusion, I simply disagree with you about the comic symbolism of flannel. To me, flannel is not so much an inherently silly fabric—it's fine when worn by farmers and lumberjacks —as a fabric that takes on a mirth-inducing character when worn in an inappropriate environment, such as an office. Much as I would like to take back what I have said about flannel, I cannot in conscience do so. Alexander the Great would not have worn flannel to work. Napoleon Bonaparte would not have worn flannel to work. And I doubt very much that Franklin Delano Roosevelt, may he rest in peace, would have worn flannel to work. In fact, just thinking about the Little General dressed up in flannel at the Battle of Waterloo makes me laugh.

On a personal note, I do not own any flannel clothing, as I can supply plenty of my own comic material without calling on my chemiserie for support. But I respect both the men and women who wear flannel and the men and women who make it. In writing my article, I was trying to make a wider point about the frivolous nature of Casual Fridays, not to single out your beloved fabric for abuse. If it is any consolation whatsoever, I could have said the same thing about bow ties, sarongs, and sweat pants, though here, of course, I would have been ridiculing a style of clothing rather than a fabric. In any event, I wish you all the best in your future ventures, and hope that you will take my comments in the spirit in which they were intended.

Sincerely,

Joe Queenan

Lordy, what a strange and exhilarating experience! The very idea that Nasty Ole Joe Queenan was writing letters to apologize for things he had written was nigh on inconceivable. Yet there I was, apologizing here, apologizing there, apologizing everywhere. Jeepers, that Grinch was in a sorry state!

I will not deny that my writing campaign was fatiguing. All told, I had saved 300 angry letters since 1986. Obviously, not all of them warranted an apology, or even a response. Many were from drunks, cranks, metalheads, degenerates, Republicans, or publicists. But 157 came from folks who had been hurt personally by something I had written and who would welcome some kind of explanation or clarification, if not an out-and-out apology.

I tried my best to accommodate them, but it was too time-consuming to go about things in this fashion. Every minute I devoted to writing letters apologizing to people for my iniquity was time I could have spent honoring diversity, boycotting homophobia, visualizing world peace, or not postponing joy. So in the end I decided to compose a one-size-fits-all apology and send it out to the many people who had written to express their displeasure over the years. It read:

> Dear Sir or Ms.,
>
> Recently, after many years of being a basically horrible human being, I decided to upgrade my value systems and become more like Susan Sarandon. A critical component of this moral rehabilitation is making amends for offenses I have committed in the past. Because I have written so many nasty things about so many people over the course of my career, I would have to spend the next five years writing apology letters to my victims, and that time could be put to better use trying to save the Spirit Bear. Bearing this in mind, I hope you will not be offended by my use of a form apology letter to express my feelings of remorse. Rest assured that my contrition is sincere, and that only the crushing weight of the contemplated paperwork prevents me from issuing you a more personal apology. In conclusion, whatever I may have done to you, I apologize most profusely, and I promise that it will not happen again.
>
> Specifically, I apologize for:
>
> ( )   Saying that your town was a dump.
>
> ( )   Saying that your book stunk.

( )   Saying that Pat Robertson, someone you greatly admire, has a village idiot's grin.

( )   Saying that your company provided rotten customer service.

( )   Blowing disgusting cigar smoke in people's faces while I was researching my story "The Week of Smoking Dangerously," which seems to have offended quite a few people.

( )   Accusing World Wrestling Federation Superstar Brian Pillman of firing what appeared to be a real gun at Stone Cold Steve Austin during a 1996 WWF television broadcast where Austin was trying to break into his house, when I should have realized that Pillman was actually brandishing a starter pistol, not a real gun.

( )   Saying that your client's book stunk.

( )   Saying that your company had a stupid name.

( )   Ridiculing ethical shoppers like you.

( )   Making fun of a genius in a wheelchair by suggesting that no one had ever actually read his book, and certainly not his editor.

( )   Accusing you of being a disgrace to the journalistic community, even in a joke magazine like *Business Week*.

( )   Failing to take seriously the issue of men who get abused by women.

( )   Using the offensive term "schmuck" in a story about Geraldo Rivera.

( )   Failing to write a *TV Guide* story about how overrated Courtney Cox is, even though you begged me to do it.

( )   Failing to investigate your allegation, apparently solid-
ly grounded, that a famous, married TV star was having an affair with your daughter while pretending to
support traditional Christian family values.

( )   Just generally being mean.

Once again, I apologize most profusely.
Joe Queenan

Sometimes I would customize these letters ever so slightly. Thus,
when I wrote to A.E. Hotchner, whose idiotic history of the Rolling
Stones I had ridiculed in the *Wall Street Journal* a few years earlier, I
checked off the box indicating that I had trashed his book, but added a
P.S. reading, "Though I did genuinely hate your book, I later read that
you helped persuade Paul Newman to start Newman's Own, a truly
saintly act. As a gesture of gratitude and contrition, I will never again
review any of your books, no matter how bad they are."

Though I initially found such penitence nettlesome, it eventually
became almost second nature to me. Just as a soldier finds it easier to
kill the second time, and much easier the tenth, I found that the practice of contrition easily became a habit. Yet all along I recognized there
was still another hill to climb, and it was a doozie. The second tier of
people I had been apologizing to were not out-and-out nobodies, no,
but at the end of the day, as Madonna might say, they sure as hell
weren't Madonna. If I was sincere about changing my stripes, I would
now have to apologize to someone it would make me physically ill to
apologize to. I would have to voluntarily respond to an angry letter sent
to me by a bona fide superstar. No, not just a superstar, but a superstar
of immeasurable magnitude. The kind of superstar you wouldn't
expect to write to mere mortals like me. The kind of superstar whose
letter had been hanging on my wall for the past four years, eliciting the
catcalls of the riffraff and the guffaws of the hoi polloi.

The letter in question had completely raked me over the coals in
response to a negative review of the writer's most recent novel. Inex-
plicably, even though the review had appeared in the *New York Times
Book Review*, the letter had been faxed to *Movieline* and then forwarded

to me. Believe you me, no punches where pulled, no quarter given. Specifically, I was lambasted for the following errors of judgment, decorum, or taste:

1) Giving away the entire plot to the novel in my review.

2) Falsely identifying one of the major characters in the novel as a "brothel operator," when even a casual reading of the book would have made it clear that she was the operator of a "call-girl service."

3) Falsely indentifying another character as a "local harlot," when she was in fact a "small-time actress."

4) Falsely indentifying yet another character as a "prostitute," when she was in fact "a happily married pregnant woman."

5) Being so obsessed with oral sex that I could not keep the characters straight.

6) Incorrectly declaring that the book was about "the death of the American family," when it quite obviously was not.

7) Falsely reporting that the author of the novel could not actually write, an assertion that seemed a tad farfetched given that she had sold more than 180 million copies of her 15 books in the previous 20 years.

8) Various other unforgivable screw-ups.

The novel in question was *Hollywood Kids*; the author of the letter none other than Jackie Collins. Now, after four years of staring at those fading fax pages, the time had come to respond to this missive. This is what I wrote:

> Dear Ms. Collins,
> First let me apologize for taking four-and-a-half years to respond to your letter about my review of *Hollywood Kids*. As I am not nearly as successful as you, I do not have anyone to help

with the paperwork, and so the mail can really pile up around here. Moreover, until I underwent a spiritual transformation quite recently, I never bothered to respond to any of my mail, because I was always hustling for a buck. But now I realize that answering one's mail, positive or negative, is an important part of being a professional writer.

I also realize that when you receive a letter from someone who has obviously been hurt by something that you wrote, it is absolutely essential that you take time out from your busy schedule and contact that person. That is what I am doing here. I know that you were stung by my assertion that you cannot actually write, particularly as the statement appeared in the *New York Times,* which a lot of your friends probably read. It is my heartfelt belief that this personal attack, and not my alleged reporting errors, triggered your angry missive. Let me only say in my defense that I did not say that you are incapable of writing because I was trying to be mean, but because I honestly believed it at the time. If it is any consolation at all, I said the same thing about Robert Ludlum and Stephen King, and it didn't seem to hurt their sales.

Before addressing the issue of whether or not you can actually write, I feel that I should deal with each of your objections to my review of *Hollywood Kids.* You start by saying that Cheryl Landers runs a call-girl service, but is not in the strict sense of the word a brothel operator. This is in fact a distinction without a difference, the sort of sophistic nitpicking no one would dream of engaging in on the East Coast. Cheryl Landers makes her living by supplying men with hookers. It's beneath you to try to pretend that the operator of a call-girl service is in a different business than a brothel keeper. Besides, I was using the term "brothel operator" euphemistically.

Your next objection baffles me. You deny that Rita is a "prostitute," but on page 432 of the paperback version of your book we learn that years earlier Rita had worked in a topless bar and "started doing guys on the side." Back where I come from, "doing guys on the side" is called prostitution.

You then accuse me of falsely identifying Kim Levitt as a prostitute, insisting that she is a happily married pregnant woman. I refer you to pages 81–82 of the paperback edition of *Hollywood Kids,* where we learn that Kim Levitt, while living in San Diego, had worked as a hooker. Additional information about Kim's life as a prostitute can be found on pages 95 and pages 163–166. Ms. Collins, you really must start reading the books that carry your name a bit more closely before they go to the printer. Either that, or make sure that the person who writes your angry letters to book reviewers does it for you.

You next object to my characterization of Kennedy Chase as a "hack journalist," insisting that she is "quite the opposite." Referring back to the book, I find that Kennedy Chase is the type of journalist who takes assignments she does not really want from publications she does not really respect, and then ends up having the following work appear under her byline:

Bobby Rush—a paler clone of Big Daddy, Jerry—thinks he's hot stuff, and he struts it all the way around the studio he acts like he owns. This is about the only time Bobby acts, because baring it all seems to be his skill de jour. What a great tight ass!

I'm sorry, Ms. Collins, but if Kennedy Chase does not fit the classic definition of the hack journalist, I don't know who does. And believe you me, some of my best friends are hack journalists, so I'm no rube! (Incidentally, the correct French in this paragraph should be "skill *du* jour," not "skill *de* jour." I can only hope that this is a typo.)

The single legitimate criticism of my review that you have made (and really, it is barely a quibble), is your assertion that Michael Scorsinni did not fall off the wagon when that drink was set in front of him on the airplane, but merely seemed on the verge of doing so. I apologize for this oversight, but with all the booze, drugs, and sex in your books, it's hard to keep the characters and their respective addictions straight.

As to your suggestion that I seem obsessed with oral sex

and prostitutes; frankly, in light of the characters you have created, and the amount of fee-based oral pleasure they provide
throughout your book, I feel that this is a case where the shoe is
on the other foot, and the condom is on the other member.
After all, you're the one who wrote the line, "...her mouth
descended on him, going to work like a dentist's suction tube"
(p. 182), not me.

Regarding your allegation that I "missed the point" by
describing the subject of your novel as "the death of the
American family," if this is the case, then why does the paperback edition of your book carry an excerpt from my review
reading

If we...look beyond Ms. Collins' glitzy...scaffolding, we...see
that the real subject of *HOLLYWOOD KIDS* is the death of the
American family....*HOLLYWOOD KIDS* is an admirable, ambi-
tious dissection of the...times we live in.

Since I find your objections pedantic at best, untenable at
worst, you may be wondering why I bothered to write this letter.
The answer is simple: There is, in fact, one major criticism of
my review that is entirely valid. When I said that "Jackie Collins
cannot actually write," I felt that I was being both honest and
accurate. However, determined to be fair, I recently reread
Hollywood Kids and must now admit that I overstated my case.
While for the most part I continue to find your prose mechanical
and obvious, with your dialogue frequently verging on self-parody,
every once in a while a sentence appears that stops me dead in
my tracks. Such a sentence can be found at the bottom of page
217, where you write

*His head was between Dahlia's legs, eating her pussy like he'd been on
a starvation diet.*

Having read and reread this passage, I am forced to retract
my earlier characterization of your writing style. While I still

maintain that you are incapable of consistently hitting the long ball, you are undeniably possessed of what one might describe as "intermittent genius," the god-given ability to occasionally pen a sentence that blows the reader right out of the room, if not out of the water. Your sentence about what transpires between Charlie Dollar and Dahlia (sorry, didn't catch her last name) is just one of those.

This being the case, I apologize for disparaging your ability as a writer. While I generally believe, as you apparently do, that my review helped to sell books, I fully understand why you would take offense at some of the remarks I made about your craft. I am sorry that I made them, and will not do so again.

I wish you the best of luck in all your future endeavors.

Sincerely,

Joe Queenan

The question can now be raised whether I honestly felt that the occasional appearance of sentences such as "His head was between Dahlia's legs, eating her pussy like he'd been on a starvation diet" in Jackie Collins's work invalidated my original assertion that she could not actually write. Well, were I summoned to the literary witness stand and required to swear on a stack of Bibles that Jackie Collins could write, I would not in conscience be able to do so. But in this particular case, I could not think of any SAB more random that I could possibly practice than to tell Jackie Collins that she could actually write, even though I knew that she could not, those 180 million copies worldwide notwithstanding. There was something poignant and sweet about Jackie's letter; it struck me as a cry in the dark for the kind of reassurance, respect, and even affection that all writers crave, but that most writers who have sold 180 million books worldwide can get by without. The fact that someone as famous as Jackie Collins should seek cultural redress from someone as insignificant as me provided indubitable evidence that we are all naked and alone in this cold, brutal universe, shivering on the heath, desperately awaiting succor that is almost certainly not coming. This being the case, I didn't think it was any big deal for me to lie and tell Jackie that she could write. It was a victimless crime.

• • •

By this point, I had personally or semi-personally apologized to everyone who had ever written me an angry letter demanding an apology and who had a legitimate reason for doing so. How did this make me feel? Great. One reason it made me feel great was because my decision to become a good person meant that I would no longer be writing the kinds of stories that would make people angry enough to demand an apology, so once this flurry of paperwork was attended to, I was free for the rest of my life.

Yet deep inside, I knew that my letter-writing campaign would not suffice. Yes, I had tried to do the right thing by sending all these apologies to my victims. But what about all those people I had traduced who had not sent me angry letters, yet who had still felt the lash of my lariat, the smite of my scimitar? Wasn't I obligated to make it up to them as well? And if so, how?

One morning I decided to take a vacation from self-abnegation. I'd spent the past few weeks feeling like a heel, devoting entire days to writing letters to people to apologize for being such a schmuck, and then going home to drink soy shakes and watch Whoopi Goldberg movies. This was character building, of course, but it wasn't terribly enjoyable. Once again, I was reminded of the words of Ben & Jerry: "If it's not fun, why do it?"

At some level, I knew that I was gravitating toward another phase in my spiritual regeneration. To date, I was still the caterpillar, perhaps even the larva, but not yet the butterfly, and I still had a lot of work to do on the contrition front. What form that contrition would take, I had no idea.

I sure hoped it wouldn't involve Streisand.

11. What a Tangled Web

In the fullness of time, I began to understand that if I was serious about being a good person, it wouldn't suffice to write checks to Greenpeace and cancel my amoral long-distance phone service and shun fur-lined mittens and drink wheatgrass shakes. Nor was it enough to stop writing horrid things about people. Or to send personal apologies to people I had offended, for that was a private act of contrition, and the time had come for ashes and sackcloth —public remorse. If I was serious about atoning for the suffering I had inflicted, it was high time I publicly apologized to all the people I had traduced over the years. It was time to set up the Contrition Website.

The idea struck me when I logged on to www.confess.net, which is an Internet confessional site where people can admit to horrible things they have done in their lives. The person who had confessed just before me had written: "I beat up old ladies." Basically I had come here to dip my toe in the rivers of regret, rehearsing the more abject acts of public remorse that would come in the future. Accordingly, I wrote the words, "I made jokes about Barbra Streisand's nose long after such humor was fashionable." In fact, I did not think this was a particularly serious offense, but I needed to get the penitence ball rolling somehow. It quickly became obvious, however, that such faceless, anonymous expressions of remorse were fundamentally meaningless. What this situation called for was serious, public self-flagellation.

For a number of reasons, a website made perfect sense. When I first conceived the idea of doing a full mea culpa, I felt that the appropriate thing would be to personally contact each of the victims of my maliciousness and issue a heartfelt apology, not unlike Bill Clinton's March 1999 apology to various Third World nations for assorted crimes inflicted on them over the years by despicable Americans. But ultimately this proved impractical. Because I had insulted or slandered more than 2,500 individuals, institutions, corporations, municipalities, philanthropic groups, and nations over the course of my career, it would have taken me years to carry out such a program, if only because people's addresses are hard to track down and I had no idea how to go about apologizing to entire nations such as Nigeria or Belgium.

Therefore, I eventually settled upon the infinitely more efficacious, but no less sincere, solution of setting up my own website where I would list all the unconscionably unpleasant things I had said about various people and groups, express my heartfelt regret, and then take measures (perhaps an ad in *Variety,* or a website address printed on the screen during my next appearance on television) to apprise the public of the site's existence. The main principle I adopted in setting up said website was that I would limit my apologies, with precious few exceptions, to people who were famous, because obscure people who get insulted in national publications should be thankful that anyone even noticed that they existed.

Thus, although I had taken many potshots at hack writers, flacks, obscure journalists, low-profile businessmen, and assorted do-gooders over the years, I did not intend to put the details on my website. For one, it might seem like I was capriciously opening old wounds. Two, ordinary people or remorse aficionados visiting my website would have no idea who they were, and therefore couldn't care less what I said about them. Third, and most important, the amount of damage inflicted on a person by being worked over in print is directly proportional to his fame. The famous bleed more than the obscure; the rich bleed more than the poor. *Quod erat demonstrandum.*

Because of the sheer volume of ill will involved, it still would not be possible for me to apologize to everyone. This underscores a more important point. To apologize to everyone was to apologize to no one. To say I was sorry for everything was to say I was sorry for nothing. Moreover, people deserved to be apologized to in descending order of apologability, with secular saints like Jimmy Carter right near the top and people like Charlie Sheen near the bottom. Finally, I decided that I would initially apologize only to those most in need of apology and then get to the rest of the people later.

Let me make it clear from the outset that I had already decided there were certain people I would never apologize to, no matter what. Here is a partial list of these individuals:

Geraldo Rivera. Mickey Rourke. Michael Milken. Anyone on Wall Street. Garth. Republicans. Barbara Walters. John Tesh, Michael Bolton, Andrew Lloyd Webber, Kenny G, Germans.

Other people I would deal with on a case-by-case basis. For example, there was no need to apologize for anything I had ever said about Tori Spelling, Chuck Norris, or the people who starred in MTV's *The Real World*. Obviously, all of these people were tools of Satan. Similarly, in a 1998 *Playboy* article about cloning, I said that the scene where the two Patrick Swayzes—one alive, one dead—appear on-screen at the beginning of *Ghost* "constitutes the strongest argument ever devised against the cloning of human beings." I was sticking with that opinion, as would anyone who saw *Roadhouse*. If the price of sanctity meant that I had to start apologizing to people like Patrick Swayze, then the price of sanctity was too steep.

Here's what the website (www.geocities.com/joemexcuse) looked like:

Welcome to the Joe Queenan Contrition Website. After many years as an irredeemably horrible human being, I have set up this website in order to publicly apologize to people as well as places I have capriciously mistreated in print over the past thirteen years. Over the past few months, I have painstakingly reviewed every word I have written, keeping my eye peeled for fulsome calumnies, unconscionable slurs, and gratuitous insults. If I treated a person unfairly, or went out of my way to be mean to a city, state, country, or even profession, I have listed the specific insult and apologized for it.

Thank you for visiting my site.

Irresponsible Journalism for Which I Would Like to Apologize Most Profusely

Allen, Joan. In a 1998 *Guardian* story in which I tried to re-create the key party in *The Ice Storm* by inviting my friends and neighbors over to swap spouses, I said that the problem with the film was that nobody really wanted to go home with the character played by Joan Allen. Specifically, I quoted a friend who remarked: "Nobody wants to sleep with someone who looks like Richard Nixon's wife." This is not true. I know lots of people who would like to sleep with somebody who looks like Pat Nixon. They should be so lucky.

Bag people. In a 1993 *Spy* photo-essay entitled "In Search of Arrogance," I went back in time ten years and spent a day as a revolting Yuppie (yellow tie, red suspenders, Gordon Gekko hair, a line of coke in the bathroom). Though most of my exploits were quite innocent and good-natured, I did invite an authentic bag person into my stretch limousine for a glass of champagne to toast Ronald Reagan's tax cuts. This was an unforgivably mean thing to do, though in my defense, it was then-*Spy* editor Tony Hendra's idea, not mine.

Baldwin, Alec. In a 1995 *Chief Executive* article I said that actors who had appeared in as many bombs as Alec Baldwin should keep their mouths shut about parrot smuggling in the Amazon when they came on *Late Night with David Letterman* to plug their latest D.O.A. film. A classic example of mixing cultural apples with ethical oranges.

Basinger, Kim. *See* Baldwin, Alec.

Ben. *See* Ben & Jerry.

Ben & Jerry. From 1987, when I first wrote about them in *Barron's*, until 1988, when I wrote about them in *Chief Executive*, I never once missed an opportunity to call them jerk-offs, or something to that effect, hauling down thousands of dollars in the process. Without citing verse and chapter, let me say only this: *Mea culpa, mea culpa, mea maxima culpa.*

Bergen, Candice. In a 1994 *American Spectator* review of *A Talent for Genius: The Life and Times of Oscar Levant*, I noted that aspiring photojournalist Candice Bergen was the last person to see the troubled genius alive, and suggested that if Levant had ever seen her act he would probably have died sooner. In fact, I had no way of knowing this, and was just being mean.

Blind people. In a 1994 *Movieline* story entitled "See No Evil," I said that "Blindness is an extremely depressing subject, because blindness itself is a physical condition which has no real upside." Oh, really? Then how do you explain Homer? Milton? Borges? Feliciano? Here, I was guilty of blatant sightism. In my defense, I did not expect any blind people to ever find out what I had written in this story, but that is not an excuse.

Bogosian, Eric. In a 1993 *Movieline* article entitled "Ham Radio," I applauded a toothless Nazi for having the good sense to go downtown and murder the annoying deejay / complete asshole played by Bogosian, the famed sit-down comic, in Oliver Stone's muscular *Talk Radio*. As any schoolchild knows, neo-Nazis should never be encouraged to leave the house, not even when they are fictional, not even when the encouragement is obviously meant as a joke. Moreover, if I in any way created the impression that I thought Bogosian himself was a complete asshole, and not simply a gifted monologist playing a complete asshole, I apologize from the very bottom of my heart.

Bono. In a 1989 *Forbes* article, I ridiculed the gifted U2 vocalist for publicly quoting Albert Camus, even though I knew deep down inside that Camus was a great writer, and I was just using the French as a prop in a cheap joke. This is an example of what the French philosopher Jean-Paul Sartre once referred to as "bad faith."

Brawley, Tawana. In a 1990 *Wall Street Journal* review of *Outrage: The Story Behind the Tawana Brawley Hoax,* I applauded the authors for proving beyond the shadow of a doubt that Tawana Brawley was a brazen liar. Since that time, I have come to understand that while the facts of the case may be in dispute, the Tawana Brawley incident is imbued with a metaphorical truth that resonates far beyond the parameters of conventionally perceived reality. In this sense, she is very much like Rigoberta Menchu or Mumia Abu-Jamal: not literally a victim of the particular outrages that she claimed to have suffered, but a victim of broader, more transcendent crimes that exist primarily in a nebulous zone of cultural magic realism.

Carradine, Keith. In a 1993 *Movieline* article entitled "Baby Love," I referred to Carradine as "a corpse masquerading as an actor." Though a tad inanimate, Carradine is actually a very fine actor who plays corpses because they are probably the only roles he ever gets offered.

Carter, Jimmy. Over the years I have so said so many cruel things about the finest ex-president this country has ever known that I would need an entire chapter to enumerate them. But if I had to pick one particular article whose transparent malevolence most makes me cringe today it would be the 1997 *Forbes ASAP* piece in which I blamed Carter for the rise of "failure chic" in America. In it, I said that honoring an unsuccessful president who had transformed himself into a successful ex-president was like honoring "the greatest unsuccessful airplane pilot in history." Today, I take it all back. For like Mr. Carter, I would rather be right than president.

Cavett, Dick. In a 1993 *Playboy* article about famous ass-kissers, I included the former talk-show host with Truman Capote, Andy Warhol, Joe McGinnis, and Lt. Columbo in a category entitled "Bootlickers Who Bite." This was my editor's idea, not mine: I have always admired Cavett and would never go out of my way to insult him. This is an example of the editorial ineptness that can afflict the freelance writer when he is juggling too many assignments at any one time and doesn't get around to revising his galleys.

Cher jokes in general. In a 1994 *Movieline* article about blindness, I said that Laura Dern's being blind had one upside: "It shields her from the awful discovery that she may soon have Cher for a mother-in-law." In a 1995 *Movieline* article about celebrity exercise videos, I joked about Cher's pudginess, suggesting that the backing song "Born to be Wild" was less appropriate than "Born to Be Wide." In a 1996 *Movieline* article about unlikely female lawyers, I referred to Cher as "the only female in the history of the universe who could possibly introduce Sonny Bono as the second-dumbest man she ever married." And in a 1990 *Movieline* article entitled "If You Can't Say Something Nice, Say It in Broken English," I said that Cher's Italian accent in the film *Moonstruck* was "an act of cultural genocide every bit as odious as Laurence Olivier's Jewish accent in *The Jazz Singer*," and as such had inflicted more damage on proud Italian Americans than "a million bad Mafia movies, 137,876,546 Joe Garagiola commercials, a life's supply of stale cannoli." In all of these cases, I was exaggerating ever so slightly, simply because Cher is without peer as a literary sight gag. In fact, although I think her gruff singing is appalling, I have always found Cher to be a surprisingly competent and often charming actress and only made these remarks because I needed some cheap laughs. This is another fine example of what the French philosopher Jean-Paul Sartre once referred to as "bad faith."

Civil War buffs. In a 1993 installation of the *Spy* "Admit It! It Sucks!" series, I said the Civil War was a load of crap, gratuitously lampooning the national nightmare in which a more perfect union was forged in the crucible of blood, as brother was pitted against brother while freedom rang. Making fun of this epic conflict, the Virginia state industry, is not funny.

Davidovich, Lolita. In a 1994 *Guardian* review of *Intersection*, I described Ms. Davidovich as being perfectly believable in the role of a young woman equipped with two ears through which one could direct a flashlight's rays with no trouble whatsoever. This was actually a line I'd been planning to use in a story about Melanie Griffith, and it had just been lying around for months because Ms. Griffith didn't have any movies out at the time, so I stuck it in there without any real concern for whether it was appropriate or not.

Differently abled athletes. In a 1997 *Wall Street Journal* op-ed piece, I ridiculed the locomotively challenged golfer Casey Martin, suggesting that disabled hockey players should be outfitted with electronic snowboards, goalies should be allowed to use wheelchairs, and worn-out baseball players should be allowed to ride golf carts in the outfield. Cheap and obvious.

Dreyfuss, Richard. In a 1996 *Washington Post* op-ed piece, I wished out loud that the director of *Mr. Holland's Opus* had ended his film the same way as *Braveheart*, with Richard Dreyfuss getting his entrails ripped out while a cast of thousands cheered. For the love of Mike, I don't know what got into me here.

Drunks. In a 1987 *Newsweek* "My Turn" column entitled "Too Late To Say 'I'm Sorry'," I trashed recovering boozehounds, most specifically my dad. After the story ran, *Newsweek* forwarded a box filled with 1,000 letters, 80 from wives and children of alcoholics who loved the story, 920 from livid recovering alkies, some vowing retribution. My dad himself actually admired the story, admitting that AA's apology "step" was a stupid idea. Nevertheless, there is no excuse for being this cruel to the millions of recovering gin monkeys who make up this great nation.

Dwarves. *See* Sting.

Eunuchs. In a 1993 *Movieline* article entitled "For Members Only," I advised vindictive women to consult the 1988 Anglo-Yugoslavian film *Stealing Heaven*, as well as the 1976 Japanese-French film *In the Realm of the Senses*, both of which illustrate "how to quickly, effectively castrate a man." Providing these kinds of detailed signposts to aberrant people is no different from those companies that publish books teaching people how to commit murder or assemble homemade nuclear weapons. Sure, the information is already in the public domain. But people like me should know better than to wave a red flag in front of a raging bull. Or heifer.

Farrow, Mia. In a 1997 *Toronto Globe & Mail* review of her autobiography, I questioned the intelligence of a woman (Mia) who would marry a man (Frank Sinatra) who was once married to a woman (Ava Gardner) who'd had an affair with her (Mia's) father. And then hook up with Woody Allen. In the end, I described her as "immensely likable but almost actionably dumb." This was not nice, and it certainly wasn't news. I also referred to her "United Colors of Benneton children" in a 1993 *Movieline* article entitled "Baby Love." The first rule of good journalism is: You never drag the kids into it. Sorry, Mia.

French, The. Made $13,000 between 1988 and 1998 mocking them in various publications, even though I go there on vacation every summer and actually like the ornery bastards. This is another example of what Jean-Paul Sartre once refered to as "bad faith."

Gates, Bill. In a 1996 *American Spectator* review of his book *The Road Ahead*, I called him a fake populist and poked fun at his stupid sweaters, even though I had made a small fortune investing in Microsoft. This is yet another example of what Jean-Paul Sartre once referred to as "bad faith."

God. In a 1998 *American Spectator* article, I wondered why God never intervened personally in the careers of professional football players like Reggie White and Randall Cunningham until *after* they stopped playing for the Philadelphia Eagles. And in a 1994 *Movieline* article entitled "And Then There Were Nuns," I said that because of her work in *The Singing Nun*, Debbie Reynolds had nailed down the position of "Actress appearing in a nun movie on whom Almighty God is least likely to show mercy at the Last Judgment." In the first case, I was merely being cheeky, since we all know that God writes straight in crooked lines. As for Debbie Reynolds's fate, that was merely wishful thinking.

Harper, Valerie. In a 1993 *Movieline* article, I cautioned that the 1984 film *Blame It on Rio* "contains rabies jokes and Valerie Harper." Valerie Harper had never done anything to warrant this kind of abuse.

Hookers. In a 1991 *Movieline* article entitled "Don't Try This at Home," I tried to impersonate Richard Gere in *Pretty Woman* by asking an 8th Avenue hooker if she would accompany me to a dinner with the CEO of a company I was taking over and pretend to be my ultra-sophisticated companion. Working girls don't need this kind of crap.

Hoosiers. In my 1992 book *Imperial Caddy*, I described the great state of Indiana as a festering hotbed of weirdness, incubating such monsters as Jim Jones, John Dillinger, Michael Jackson, and Axl Rose. The truth is, the same intellectually threadbare argument could have been made about any state in the Union.

Jazz. Said that it sucked in the 1994 *Spy* series "Admit It! It Sucks!"

and although I thought the article was quite good-natured and made some interesting points by questioning various assumptions and received wisdom, a lot of people felt that it had a racist subtext. In my defense, I should point out that famous white musicians such as Chet Baker, Gerry Mulligan, Stan Getz, and Bucky Pizzarelli were prominent targets of my venom, and that I did honestly believe at the time that jazz blew it right out the ass, but now that I've listened to a few Chick Corea records I know otherwise.

Jerry. *See* Ben & Jerry.

Men with small penises. In a 1997 *Men's Health* article entitled "An Inch Too Far," I'd stated categorically that the only people who should even think of getting penis extensions were "men cursed with microphalluses, victims of car accidents, or editors at *Vanity Fair.*" Oh, you catty bitch!!!

Meredith, Courtney, Megan, Shawn, Jason, Erik, and Scott. Throughout the past decade, I continually made fun of children saddled with these unfortunate names, even though it clearly wasn't their fault.

Montand, Yves. In a 1997 *Movieline* article about movie stars who became famous by getting the shit kicked out of them, I said that "one of my greatest regrets in life was that I never got to see debonair Yves Montand lying in the gutter getting his head stomped on by malevolent street urchins." In fact, this had never been one of my great regrets; I barely knew who the guy was. I only said it because you can always get a laugh by making fun of the French.

Mother Nature. Innumerable *ad florinem* and *ad fauninem* attacks over the years, but the worst was my 1993 *Washington Post* piece in which I said that mankind's systematic rape of the planet over the past two hundred years was just recompense for millions of years of abuse —cholera, smallpox, earthquakes, the Black Death, hurricanes, floods, AIDS—by Mother Nature. Completely indefensible twaddle.

Movement, The Men's. In a 1992 article, I advised readers of *Chief Executive* to "purchase lots of assault weapons and not be afraid to use them." Unconscionable.

Native Americans. In a 1993 *Movieline* article entitled "Seeing Red," I said that the lowest point in the history of the red man was not the massacre at Wounded Knee or Sand Creek or the Trail of Tears but the release of the 1964 film *Cheyenne Autumn* in which Ricardo Montalban plays an Indian chieftain. Though my intentions were entirely honorable, this kind of insensitive remark trivializes the epic saga of the American Indian.

O'Connor, Sinead. Called her a "short, bald, distaff Bono" in a 1992 issue of *Us*. Here I was guilty of sizeism, lookism, and hypocrisy, since I own all of Sinead's records and was just looking for cheap laughs. This is yet another example of what Jean-Paul Sartre once referred to as "bad faith."

Out-of-shape pregnant women. In a 1995 *Movieline* article entitled "Sweating with the Stars," I sneered at *Kathy Smith's Pregnancy Workout*, remarking that watching the women shimmy and jiggle in the video was like watching *White Female Sumo Wrestlers' Funniest Home Videos*. Women are the mothers of our children and the hope of the planet and should never, ever be laughed at, no matter how preposterously skimpy their leotards.

Panush, Don. For a 1987 *Spy* prank, I visited one of those storefront legal offices in New York City and told Mr. Panush that I wanted to do a $35 million leveraged buyout of a White Plains firm that made the fibrous underpadding used in prisons and mental institutions. I suppose it was an amusing enough story at the time, but basically I was just fucking with the guy, who didn't really need this kind of crap, so I apologize.

Peter, Paul & Mary, et al. In a 1988 *New Republic* article entitled "If *I* Had a Hammer," I theorized that the Nixon administration had made a secret deal with the antiwar movement to pull out of Vietnam if Peter, Paul & Mary, Richie Havens, Joan Baez, and others of their ilk went away forever. The article specifically referred to Peter, Paul & Mary as "monsters." Worse still, in a 1996 article for the online content provider *Mr. Showbiz*, I criticized Amtrak customers for not lynching either Peter or Paul—I can no longer remember which—when he started playing folk songs on a delayed Washington–New York Metroliner. Once again, going after a gnat—well, three gnats—with a thermonuclear device.

Rifkin, Jeremy. In a 1992 review of Rifkin's *Beyond Beef: The Rise and Fall of the Cattle Culture* entitled "Silence of the Cows," I sneered at his theory that methane gas emitted from millions of cow butts was endangering the planet. This was a very bad thing to do, because environmentalists should never be ridiculed, no matter how shaky the scientific foundations of their arguments. Therefore, even though this review appeared in *Across the Board,* a magazine which almost no one ever saw, I am deeply sorry for my gratuitous cruelty.

Rushdie, Salman. In a 1989 *American Spectator* article, I said that the reason I was the last American writer to come out in defense of the menaced novelist was not because I was afraid of Islamic terrorists, but because I was out of town at the time, and also because I thought we were supposed to go in alphabetic order, so I was waiting for Joyce Carol Oates and the Podhoretzes to weigh in. Making a fast $250 off the misfortunes of a writer far greater than me is odious, especially when the money comes from a virulently right-wing publication like *The American Spectator.*

Sarandon, Susan. In a mean-spirited 1989 *Rolling Stone* article entitled "Miss Congeniality," I ridiculed the actress's political convictions by noting: "Like many people who have villas in Italy, apartments in New York, and good jobs in Hollywood, Sarandon supports innumerable political causes. These include women, homeless women, homeless people, victims of Central American political repression, AIDS victims, and Nicaraguan mothers. Environmentally sensitive readers, and manatee readers tired by the immense amount of press coverage more colorful aquatic species seem to get, will be heartened to know that at no point has Sarandon expressed any concern about the whales." Here, let's face it, I was just being a snide-assed bully.

Security guards. In a 1988 *New York* front-of-the-book piece, I eviscerated an overworked, underpaid security guard at the bag check counter of the New York Public Library's main branch who refused to give me back my knapsack because I had presented the wrong claim check. Even though I could tell him everything that was in the bag—my checkbook with my name on it, a white comb, a green case holding a dental retainer, a *Newsweek* story with my photograph atop it—he would not turn it over. At the time, I pilloried him as an idiot. In fact, he was probably just a hard-working immigrant stiff who was thrown off his guard by my staggering powers of prestidigitation, and I may even have antagonized him deliberately because I knew there was $800 in a *New York* story if I could make him look like a real idiot.

Seeger, Pete. *See* Peter, Paul & Mary.

Sheen, Charlie. In a 1991 *Movieline* article entitled "Young Gums," I discussed a scene in the film *Young Guns* in which the veteran actor Brian Keith, while concealed in an outhouse, made more of an impression than Sheen, Kiefer Sutherland, Lou Diamond Phillips, and Emilio Estevez did while they were actually on the screen. Even when I was writing this, I knew that it was not true. True, the invisible Keith—never a lord of the boards, mind you—did out-act Sutherland, Phillips, and Estevez while concealed in the shithouse, but Charlie Sheen generally held his own. I only included him with the others for the sake of comic effect and because a joke like that works better when it's monolithic. Roger Ebert would never have played as fast and loose with the facts as me, which is why he is where he is today.

Sorbonne, The. In a 1990 *Movieline* profile of Melanie Griffith entitled "Dark Side of the Moon," I poked fun at the venerable French academic institution, founded in 1554, by repeating Griffith's 1973 announcement that she planned to go to the Sorbonne and study philosophy. I knew perfectly well at the time that the Sorbonne does not accept students like Melanie Griffith and was simply making another joke at the expense of the French. This is perhaps the finest example of what Jean-Paul Sartre once referred to as "bad faith."

Spano, Vincent. Too many nasty remarks to list here, but the worst popped up in my 1993 *Movieline* article about *Alive*. This is a film about a bunch of Uruguayan rugby players who crash in the Andes and are forced to eat one another in order to survive. While seated in a theater watching the film, I hollered out to Ethan Hawke and the other victims of the crash that they should "eat Vincent Spano first," as he was by far the worst actor in the movie. Such behavior in a motion picture theater is totally unacceptable, and will not be repeated.

Stalin, Joseph. In a 1991 *Movieline* article about Barbra Streisand entitled "Sacred Cow," I suggested that if the lefty activist with the bad perm played by Babs in *The Way We Were* was handing out leaflets on behalf of the Soviet Union in the early 1950s, the person she was actually going to bat for was Joseph Stalin himself. This was a terribly unfair accusation to make, since it trivializes the struggle of the Russian peoples and their glorious Revolution, and I apologize to the deceased Soviet strongman for such a calumny.

Sting. In a 1991 *Movieline* article, I poked fun at the rock star for being "out-acted by a dwarf" in *The Bride*. Why, I now ask myself, is it so odd for a singer-turned-actor to be out-acted by someone shorter than him? Meryl Streep is shorter than Arnold Schwarzenegger, yet no one thinks it humiliating for him to be out-acted by her. Clearly, I only made this remark because it was the meanest thing I could think to say about Sting. But in doing so, I displayed gross insensitivity toward the diminutive actor David Rappaport, to whom I now also apologize for gratuitous sizeism.

Turner, Kathleen. In a 1992 *Movieline* article about movies hamstrung by incomprehensible story lines, I ridiculed Turner's performance in *V.I. Warshawski*, noting that she played a "fat private investigator." I have since gone back and watched the movie again. She wasn't *that* fat.

Un Pueblo Unido Jamas Sera Vencido. In a 1997 *Wall Street Journal* review of *Heretic's Heart: A Journey through Spirit and Revelation*, I blasted Margot Adler, National Public Radio's New York bureau chief, for reading the manuscript of her book to her ninety-year-old pinko dad while he lay dying in the hospital. One of the first things they teach you in journalism school is: Never make fun of the dying, even if they are unreconstructed old commies. Sadly, I never went to journalism school.

Westheimer, Dr. Ruth. In a 1996 story in *Men's Health*, I said that if you were going to follow Dr. Ruth's advice and appear to your lover dressed only in a top hat, you should not do this if you had a body like Dr. Ruth's. Though the intent here was clearly humorous, the effect was unnecessarily cruel.

Winters, Shelley. In an 1994 *Movieline* article entitled "See No Evil," I asserted that the one advantage of being blind was that "the blind get to go through their entire lives without ever seeing Shelley Winters." I have no idea how I could be so mean, and besides this was a callous recycling of a joke I'd already made about Cher in *Mask*. Very unprofessional.

Yablans, Frank. In a 1992 *Movieline* article entitled "Clerical Errors," I suggested that the producer of the ferociously anti-Catholic film *Monsignor* was almost certainly going to hell because of his role in both the making and the distribution of this supremely offensive motion picture. In fact, I haven't the foggiest idea what God has in store for Mr. Yablans. I was simply guessing.

Young, Sean. In 1989, I interviewed the comely but ill-starred starlet at her Greenwich Village apartment for *Rolling Stone*. When I arrived, Young was having her weekly algebra lesson with a math tutor, and I suggested in my article that because she was having so much trouble with the powers that be in the movie industry she might in fact be preparing for a second career as "America's most fetching algebra teacher." I also obliquely poked fun at her recently acquired math skills. This was totally unfair. I was terrible at math in high school, and would have no way of knowing whether Sean Young was an idiot or a direct spiritual heir of Euclid. It was just another opportunity for a cheap laugh at somebody else's expense, and I apologize.

People I Specifically Do Not Want to Apologize to

O. J. Simpson, Don Simpson, Adolf Hitler, manufacturers or users of leaf blowers, editors of small literary magazines like *The Lightning Herald: Un Journal de Poetes Terribles*, gamines, Chris Berman, Elizabeth Hurley, English houseguests, washed-up child actors, people who bring ostrich farms public, the 1964 Phillies, subscribers to cigar magazines, knowledge workers, focus groups, editorial-page writers who blame everything on *hubris*, Joan Didion, eco-tourists, journalists who make their living writing about what other journalists write about, Mary Beth Whitehead, people who write books with the words "ninja," "samurai," or "tao" in the title, Marshal Petain, Neville Chamberlain, the New York Rangers, Graydon Carter, Michael Jackson, the New York Metropolitan Transportation Authority, Brooke Shields, Steve Guttenberg, Rod Stewart, Ahmad Rashad, Regis Philbin, LaToya Jackson, Liz Taylor, Kathie Lee Gifford, Heidi Fleiss, cyber-geeks, people who start their own mail-order religions, people who publish their own "ironic" newsletters, copywriters, the guy who wrote *Leadership Secrets of Attila the Hun* and then took my words out of context to hype the book, maverick CEOs, literary agents, *Who's Who in America*, demographics experts, Faith Popcorn, overpriced thrift shops, comic-book enthusiasts, people who think the Mayan civilization was founded by extraterrestrials, John Tower, all contemporary American short-story writers, most satanists, MBA candidates, derivatives salesmen, the grommet industry, Grace Jones, Brigitte Neilsen, Eric Roberts, Donovan, Erik Estrada, Kathleen Sullivan, deconstructionists, Stanley Bing, multiculturalists, Pete Petersen, Jude Wanniski, Lee Iacocca, Chuck Norris, Shirley MacLaine, Ali McGraw, Sammy Davis Jr., Deepak Chopra, Ed McMahon, Raquel Welch, Michael Medved, Joe Pesci, Greg Kinnear, New York Jets fans, Jane Fonda, Tony Curtis, Madonna, Jerry Glanville, Robin Cook, *Reader's Digest,* Dennis Levine, white *New York Times* rock critics who pretend not to hate rap music, Brent Musberger, Ricardo Montalban, Patrick Swayze, Fergie, Sharon Stone, Iron Butterfly, Chevy Chase, Goldie Hawn, Grand Funk Railroad, Joe Piscopo, David Spade, Adam Sandler, Sylvester Stallone, Joe Eszterhas.

People I Did Not Have to Be So Mean to, But Was Not So Mean That They Deserve a Detailed Apology

David Crosby, Penelope Anne Miller, Don Knotts, the guy who made the *Benji* movies, professional golfers, Tim Conway, Tony Robbins, Nick Nolte, Dionne Warwick, Christopher Reeve, Carol Alt, Paulina Porizkova, Kathy Ireland, Cindy Crawford, models in general, Bill Pullman, Peter Gallagher, John Travolta, Dennis Quaid, Aidan Quinn, the Chieftains.

Places I Did Not Have to Be Quite So Mean to

Iowa, Edmonton, Paraguay.

Places I Specifically Do Not Want to Apologize to

Raleigh-Durham, Dallas, Branson, Mo., the South in general.

If I have written about you and your name does not appear above, it either means that I do not believe that what I wrote about you warrants an apology or that you are not famous enough to apologize to. If you feel that you do deserve an apology or are famous enough to receive an apology, please state your case and e-mail me at joemexcuse @hotmail.com. Please include all pertinent details about the publication in which you were insulted, the date of the insult, and the page number of the insult. At the earliest possible opportunity I will review your grievance, and if your complaint is found to have merit, I will issue you a personal apology by E-mail or mail (please enclose SASE) and a public apology the next time I update the site.

I thank you in advance for your interest.

12. Second Thoughts

Just because my website was now ready for the big roll-out didn't mean I couldn't find other ways to make up for obnoxious things I had done in the past. Take, for example, my relationship with the Third World. One afternoon I read a story about Jubilee 2000, the protest concert that was to be held in June 1999 in Cologne, Germany, an extremely unlikely locale to find do-gooders, at least in this century. The protest concert was organized by a variety of churches and other socially conscious groups, and was slated to coincide with the G8 summit of the world's leading industrial nations. The idea behind the concert was to persuade the world's wealthiest nations to write off the debt of the world's poorest nations as a sort of Happy New Millennium gift.

Although I recognized that in the abstract this was a wonderful gesture, I immediately had grave reservations about the economic ramifications of such a proposal. Forgiving debt in many Third World countries was certain to encourage the thieves who had bankrupted these nations in the first place to go on with their plundering, safe in the knowledge that the rich countries would bail them out further down the line. Somewhere I had heard Russia described as a kleptocracy, where there was literally no point in letting the International Monetary Fund pour in capital infusions because the money was only going to end up in the hands of corrupt government leaders and gangsters. Another problem was that First World investors who had purchased the debt of impoverished nations, rather than governments, would bear the brunt of this widescale debt repudiation. Without rigorously determining precisely who was going to be footing the bill for this Third World bail-out, this did not seem like a very good idea at all.

Perhaps my biggest reservation was that Michael Stipe, lead singer of REM, had offered the services of his band at the protest concert. I have always found REM a fascinating band musically, but intellectually a bit on the dim side. Also, I was justifiably wary of any economic Marshall Plan devised by a native of Georgia. Jimmy Carter had evolved into a fine ambassador to mankind since his days in the White House, but as an economic czar he had been a complete disaster. Remember: The inflation rate hit 12.5 percent when he was president. Much as I hated to admit it, this Third World bail-out scheme seemed like the sort of well-meaning but disastrous plan Carter and his Georgia Mafia would have come up with were they still running the country.

On the other hand, the moral underpinnings of the movement to forgive Third World debt were impeccable, so I immediately began thinking of ways that I could do on the micro level what the churches and protesters and REM were trying to do on the global level. Basically, I decided that I would immediately forgive any debts owed to me by any people from Third World countries. Unfortunately, I don't know any people from the Third World because I am a horrible Yuppie and live in the suburbs. The best I could think of was to give the Mexican waiters in my local diner an extra-large tip.

Then one afternoon I realized that the peoples of the Third World did have a bone to pick with me. In a December 1998 article in *The American Spectator*, I had maliciously slandered the fine people of Paraguay by describing their national heartbreak when they finished second to the Cameroons in the annual competition for most corrupt nation in the world.

"Paraguay never wins anything," moaned Esteban Porforio, the fictitious president of Paraguayans for an Even Worse Paraguay, a special-interest group that I also invented. "We have no movie stars, no rock stars, no world-class athletes, no monuments, no history, no economy. Nobody even knows where this country is. Winning that award for corruption would have meant a lot to the people of Paraguay. It would have put us on the map."

As soon as I had finished rereading this vicious article, I grabbed a train into the city, stopped off at a florist's, and delivered a lush bouquet to the Paraguayan embassy with a note reading

"Sorry about that *American Spectator* article.
Best of luck in all your endeavors.
Vaya con dios, muchachos."

That made me feel much better.

On the home front, I was starting to reap the benefits of my new-found contriteness. Allan Fine, president of that shirt company down in Tennessee, called to tell me how much he appreciated my letter, and what a great writer I was, and also asked for my shirt size so he could send me "a couple of shirts" allowing me to see for myself that flannel was anything but a "silly" fabric. Tom Shales had written from Alabama to thank me for refunding him the price of *Red Lobster*, adding, "If your next book is as thoughtful as your correspondence, I shall read it with pleasure." Oh, my next book would be thoughtful all right! Meanwhile, everybody in creation was sending me thank-you notes for my generous contributions on behalf of the Siberian tiger, the timber wolf, the sperm whale, the Spirit Bear. These days, I was feeling pretty darn good about my place in the grand scheme of things.

Unfortunately, not everybody on this small planet was adhering to the game plan as closely as I was. Some people I had come to love and respect were starting to let me down. Kim Basinger, for example. Imagine how I felt the morning I awoke and read in the *New York Post* that animal rights activist Basinger had appeared in a movie using circus elephants and a dog "shot up with dope." Having only recently persuaded my son to give me one of his teeth to support one of Kim's husband's causes, and having suffered through *My Stepmother Is an Alien*, *The Real McCoy*, and *Pret-à-Porter* just to be nice to Kim, I felt terribly betrayed that Alec's right hand did not know what Kim's left hand was doing. As I continued to read the article, I felt a bit better about Kim's actions, since the circus in question was not a big-time operation like Barnum & Bailey's, but a more genteel outfit called Brian's Circus, so it was unlikely that the elephants had been mistreated. I decided that I would take steps to ascertain the truth of these allegations against Basinger. And if it turned out that Kim had actually appeared in a film where elephants were mistreated, I was going to stop supporting her career and would also write to the Radiation and Public Health Project and ask for my son's tooth back. If Kim and Alec were going to talk the talk, they had to walk the walk.

Speaking of Kim Basinger, there was more trouble brewing with the USDA. Shortly after I gave my pro bono (no honorarium, just travel expenses, did I mention this already?) speech to that gathering of government publicists and communicators down in our nation's capital, I received a very nice note from a USDA official expressing interest in having me address the national gathering of the organization in the year 2000. Hey, if there was money, I was game. But then I read a newspaper article reporting that a genetically altered strain of corn *approved by the USDA* was killing off the lovely monarch butterfly and "may be killing other insects and doing other unseen damage to the food chain." If this was true, and I had every reason to believe that it was, then it was high time the USDA and I exchanged the Big Sayonara.

These were hardly my only problems. As time went on, I found myself baffled by the awesome complexity of leading a truly virtuous life, and by the innumerable philosophical paradoxes that confronted me every step of the way. Let me give an example. I had been playing basketball in Tarrytown since I moved there in 1983, and most of the time I'd worn sneakers manufactured by a firm that will heretofore be refered to as "Company X." For quite some time, I had been aware that Company X was a morally suspect company that operated sweatshops in the Third World and then sold its products at huge markups to inner-city kids who had been known to kill one another for garish foot-gear because they could not afford to buy it. In fact, I had even con-fronted Company X spokesman Spike Lee about this issue when I interviewed him for *Movieline* in 1996, eliciting one of his typically wheedling, half-assed responses. I used this as yet one more reason to dislike this cagey operator. As if anyone actually needed one more rea-son.

Despite my misgivings about Spike Lee's moral Gumbyness, I continued to wear Company X sneakers because

1) They give lots of support in the instep and the heel, obviating the need for orthotics.

2) They are more stylish and more durable than their competi-tors' products.

3) I do not appear in or direct commercials for Company X and thus can be held to a lower moral standard.

4) I am a deeply superstitious person who honestly believes that I play better when I wear Company X's sneakers than when I wear Reeboks or Adidas or Converse or any of that other crap.

This placed me directly in the eye of the ethical tiger once I entered the moralistic tunnel of love. As soon as I initiated my program to reconstruct my personality, I knew that I would have to get rid of all my Company X products. This was an expensive proposition, since I owned three pairs of Company X sneakers and one pair of Company X hiking shoes, but I did it, because that is what Sting would have done. Then, because I was aware that Reebok sponsored the Reebok Human Rights Awards, which helped to free political prisoners all around the world, I went out and bought a pair of Reebok basketball shoes, even though my previous experiences with that company had been unhappy (they fell apart in a hurry, they looked like battleships, they gave crummy support, I hated the Reebok logos). The result was that I felt a lot better, but looked a lot worse.

A few weeks after I started wearing the Reeboks, I ripped a muscle in my lower back while making one of my patterned drives to the basket past the hapless Greg Clary at the YMCA. The injury put me on the sidelines for a month. Obviously, I cannot say for certain that I hurt my back because the Reeboks were duds. All I know is that the only time in my life that I ripped a muscle in my back occurred when I was wearing footwear that I had purchased for moral rather than athletic reasons.

Maybe I'd hit a dead spot in the floor or maybe I'd failed to stretch properly or maybe I'm a decrepit old coot who was bound to incur an injury like this somewhere along the line. But one thing I can tell you for sure: I am never wearing another pair of Reebok sneakers to the gym and I don't give a damn how many political prisoners the company helps spring from the slammer. Whatever good I had brought into the world by not wearing Company X's products was more than canceled out by the time I spent incapacitated, time that could have been spent practicing RAKs and SABs. From that point on, I swore off both Reeboks and Company X's. I'd stick with New Balance, a company universally revered for its labor practices and concern for the environment. But I must point out that this was a decision much more easily made by a paunchy, graying forty-eight-year-old white man who doesn't have to integrate stylistic concerns into his consumer purchases than by a youthful hepcat. Had I been a twenty-year-old person of color, I would have been in a real bind. Word up: You can't take the rock to the hole and rain jumpers from the sky like Lamar Mondaine in a raggedy-ass pair of New Balances, because New Balances look like shit.

· · ·

Suddenly, after months of relatively uninterrupted bliss, I found myself beset on all sides by disappointments. One morning I got a card from Edwidge Danticat, the Haitian novelist to whom I had sent the $1,000 check after she'd been screwed by the Don Imus American Book Awards. She didn't want the money. Damn. The same day, I ran into Sam Tanenhaus, the biographer of Whittaker Chambers, whose shafting by the National Book Awards people had prompted Imus to establish his alternative awards, but who himself had never gotten a dime out of the I-Man. I felt so sorry for Sam that I was all set to sign over the $1,000 check to him. But then he told me that he had just left his job at the editorial page of the *New York Times* and taken a lucrative position at *Vanity Fair,* the publicist's best friend. In short, Sam had crossed over to the dark side. No money for him.

And there was more bad news on the ethical conundrum front. In May 1999, the Giuliani administration announced plans to sell off the sites of 112 community gardens in New York City. Though I was well aware that a series of protests had been organized to shame the mayor into reversing his policy, this was one of those situations where I chose to stay on the sidelines because my wife and I had been members of a community garden at 31st and 3rd from 1976 to 1983 and I felt that I had already done enough on the urban gardening front and should let somebody else carry the ball. Also, I did not feel like dressing up like a sunflower or a sun-dried tomato to protest the city's policy, or even to be associated with people who did, because I am Irish-American and Irish-Americans don't do things like that.

The person who chose to carry the ball in this case was none other than Bette Midler, who contributed $250,000 of her own money to a fund that bought half of the properties. This fund, the New York Restoration Project, took control of fifty-one of the parcels, and then gave an additional $1 million to a second organization, the Trust for Public Land, which used it to buy the remaining fifty-one lots. This was a wonderful gesture on Ms. Midler's part. Truly wonderful. Nevertheless, I still hated her schmaltzy records and putrid movies. One part of me—the part that was watching all those Robin Williams films and listening to all those Sting CDs—thought that the right thing to do was to go out and buy her worst records and rent her worst movies, thus lending a kind of retroactive support to her up-and-down career, enabling her to make more money that could then be used to buy more community gardens or beautify highways or subsidize a cure for AIDS or lupus.

But the other part of me had seen *The Rose* and the trailer from *For the Boys*. And the other part of me was unforgiving. It was the classic moral schism: Just because you admired John F. Kennedy, Martin Luther King, and Honest Abe didn't make "Abraham, Martin and John" any less revolting. In the end, I wished Bette all the best in her horticultural efforts. But there was no way I was renting the HBO remake of *Gypsy*. My kids would have beheaded me.

My confusion didn't stop there. One day, while paging through the National Anti-Vivisection Society's cruelty-free shopping guide, I noticed that the book was liberally adorned with photographs of cuddly little bunny rabbits. The use of such photos was entirely sensible, since rabbits are lovable animals. But ethically speaking, these graphics were suspect. Although some twenty million animals are used in scientific experiments in the United States every year, most of them are rats and mice. It appeared that the NAVS was deliberately misleading the public into thinking that rabbits were the main victims of these experiments, when this was manifestly not the case. Needless to say, I was chagrined that the NAVS should resort to the kind of deliberately misleading graphics that are typical of Madison Avenue. So I immediately decided to contact the organization and register my displeasure.

I reached for the phone. But then I had second thoughts. Several months earlier, the reader will recall, I had switched my long-distance service to Working Assets Long Distance, the San Francisco-based, left-leaning, long-distance telephone supplier that would subsidize my moral values by giving me sixty free minutes of long-distance phone calls every month that I could use to make calls registering my objection to this or that heinous corporate or ideological policy. The NAVS was located in Chicago, a toll call from Tarrytown. The question was: Would Working Assets pay for this long-distance call given that the recipient was not a ghastly right-wing organization but an entity supported by organizations such as Working Assets? And was it even appropriate to put the company in such a morally untenable position?

The answers were no and no. When I called Working Assets and asked if I could use my free five minutes a month to complain about causes that mattered to me personally, rather than to rant about the designated lefty issues decided by the phone company, the answer was no. If I wanted to complain about left-wing causes, I would have to pay for it myself at a rate of ten cents a minute. But I still felt guilty about making the call over left-of-center phone lines, so in the end I decided to write, rather than call, the NAVS. I sent them the following letter:

> Dear Sir or Ms.,
>
> Several weeks ago, I sent away for a copy of *Personal Care for People Who Care*. As soon as I had finished reading it, I threw out just about everything I had stored in my bathroom and started fresh with a big shop at the Body Shop. What was most amazing to me was that just about everything in my closets and medicine cabinet—shaving cream, toothpaste, adhesive bandages, shampoo—was made by companies that conducted experiments on animals. I will never patronize any of these companies again, so help me God.
>
> There is one thing that bothers me about your shopping guide, however. On the cover of the ninth edition can be found four photographs. One depicts a man who looks a little bit like Yankee skipper Joe Torre either sniffing or nuzzling a cat. Next to this is a photo of a cute toddler playing with a cuddly bunny rabbit. In the lower right-hand corner are a pair of generic Yuppies with a sweet-looking puppy, and next to that a little girl with yet another kitten. On the back cover is a photo of a little boy with a dog.
>
> Turning the cover page, on the inside cover I find a photo of three bunny rabbits frolicking atop and around a computer, which itself contains an image of a cuddly bunny. On the facing page is an even cuter bunny. On page 8 we come across Bunny No. 6, and bunnies also surface on pages 15, 17 (3 bunnies), 19, 46, 82, 141, 144, 168, 179, and 187. That adds up to 18 bunnies, 2 kittens, and 2 puppies.
>
> Hey, what happened to the rats? According to the Council

on Economic Priorities' *Shopping for a Better World,* approximately 20 million animals are used in lab research each year, but "the
majority are rats and mice" (page 17). And from mailings by the
American Anti-Vivisection Society, I know that birds are also
used in numerous experiments. Yet in your guide I didn't find a
single photograph of a rat, mouse, or bird.

Hey, don't get me wrong. I understand perfectly well why
you chose to gussy up your booklet with pictures of bunny rabbits rather than rats or mice. They're cute, they elicit sympathy,
it makes people gag to think of them being mistreated. That
doesn't change the fact that you are practicing deceptive advertising. What's more, by perpetuating the stereotype of bunny rabbits as being cute and cuddly (which is not the way they are perceived in Australia and in certain parts of England), you are
masking the real issue: that people should object to animal
experiments on moral grounds even if the animals are disgusting
rats. In effect, your publishing effort, which is basically intended
to save rats and mice, is trying to trick the public into thinking
that the primary victims of cruel experiments are rabbits. This is
like Amnesty International trying to save Kurdish men by sending out fund-raising solicitations festooned with photographs of
cute little political prisoners from the Rodeo Drive Nursery
School. Effective, perhaps, but not fair.

I hope you will write me and explain your position on this
matter.

Best wishes,

Joe Queenan

My disappointment at the graphically manipulative tactics of the
NAVS proved to be only the first bump on a very slippery slope. One
afternoon, as I was continuing Operation Purge the Larder, getting rid
of all the morally offensive foodstuffs stored in my refrigerator and
pantry, I noticed that my Beastliness Baedeker, *Shopping for a Better
World,* had been published in 1994. Frantically paging through the
guide, I realized that the information provided was a full five years out
of date. I immediately grabbed my phone and made a concerted effort

to resolve this problem. (Since the Council on Economic Priorities is based in New York, I did not have to use up any of my sixty free long-distance dialing minutes from Working Assets and thus did not feel morally conflicted by using donated minutes clearly earmarked to harangue the likes of Jessie Helms and Pat Robertson.)

Sadly, my worst suspicions were quickly confirmed. Identifying myself as a consumer who had recently purchased *Shopping for a Better World,* I asked why the book was five years out of date. The woman who took my call said that a new edition would be coming out later in 1999.

"But that's not fair to the companies!" I exclaimed. "Some of them may have changed their policies since 1994."

The woman sounded exasperated. She said that if I was not happy with the guide, I could send it back for a complete refund. That was hardly the point. What sense did it make for a company to alter its policies on animal testing or minority advancement or concern for the environment if it was going to have to wait five years for its actions to be recognized? After all, *Consumer Reports* did not publish evaluations of 1999 sports utility vehicles based on 1994 research. The response that I received was shocking.

"Very few of the companies have changed their policies since 1994," she informed me.

"But some of them have!" I shot back. "It's not fair, and it's not ethical to accuse companies of objectionable practices that may no longer be in effect."

"Well, you can send the book back for a full refund," she told me.

That cut it. Seething with moral indignation, I banged out an angry letter to the powers that be at the Council on Economic Priorities:

Dear Sir or Ms.,

A few weeks ago I bought a copy of *Shopping for a Better World.* As soon as I finished reading it, I began purging my medicine cabinet of products made by uncaring, insensitive, or just plain evil companies. Believe you me, a ton of shampoo, soap, toothpaste, bath oils, skin lotions, unguents, shaving cream, and other items made by firms that failed to meet your rigorous ethical criteria went right into the trash can.

But a couple of days ago, while trying to decide whether or not to throw away my TV set because the manufacturer is involved in the manufacture of products used by the military, I happened to notice that the book I was working with had been published in 1994. That means that it is now a full five years out of date. That means that any company that has changed its policies since 1994 is still being pilloried in your guide as an environmental abuser or racially insensitive or fundamentally misogynist or just plain nasty. This does not seem fair.

When I called your office last week, the woman who listened to my complaint said that if I was not happy with the book, I could send it back for a full refund. That is hardly the point. Because I am quite well fixed, I do not care about getting a refund for a picayune amount of money. What concerns me is the accuracy of the data collected in your book. When I pointed out that the book had a 1994 copyright, your employee told me that the next fully revised edition of the book would not be published until 1999.

Since this is already the year 1999, I don't think you're employing the world's most cutting-edge staff down there. But again, that is not the point. The point is the accuracy of the data being disseminated. When I suggested that it was unfair to companies that had changed their policies and practices towards minorities or gays or the environment or animal testing since 1994 to continue to identify them as polluters or bigots or animal tormentors, the woman said that very few companies had in fact changed their policies.

Not a good answer. 1) What made her so sure? And 2) even if 999 companies have not changed their policies, but one has, it still means that your book cannot be relied upon. What's more, such a cavalier editorial philosophy may even encourage bad corporate citizens to cling to their objectionable policies because they figure that there's no point in suddenly becoming good corporate citizens because it's going to take you guys five years to get around to recognizing it anyway.

Let me say that I have been a horrible, insensitive person most of my adult life (it is generally agreed that I was a pretty nice kid) but have recently made a concerted attempt to morally upgrade my personality, in part by using your book as a shopping guide. However, inaccuracy or incompetence in the service of good is not much better than accuracy or competence in the service of evil. In other words, if I'd thrown out all my GE products because you had identified them as military contractors, and then found out that they had gotten out of that business four years ago, I'd be pretty darned steamed.

In conclusion, let me reiterate that I do not want a refund, as I am unspeakably well-heeled, and suspect that you probably need the money more than I do. In fact, you might even use some of it to hire someone to answer the phones who wasn't such a numskull. What I would like is a response to my inquiry. Is it true that your guide is only published every five years? What mechanisms exist to alert consumers when previous offenders have crossed over from the realm of darkness into the kingdom of light? Have any of the companies that have changed their policies since your last publication ever given you a hard time about this issue? Threatened to sue your pants off?

In the meantime, I wish you the best of luck with all your endeavors. While I do find your publication a tad unwieldy, I understand that collating such a massive amount of data cannot be an easy task and applaud your industriousness. But I honestly hope you will think about these matters and try to get the guide published more regularly. If word got out that *Consumer Reports* hadn't updated its ratings on microwaves and sports-utility vehicles for the past five years, I honestly don't know how many people would still be subscribing to the magazine. If you get my drift.

Sincerely,

Joe Queenan

Of course, it cut me to the quick that for the second time in my career I would have to report in print that *Shopping for a Better World* was a hopelessly misconceived, methodologically benighted publication. But I had to do it. I suppose that what distressed me the most was the utterly Manichean attitude of the council—the notion that the corporate world was permanently divided into the good and the evil, and that even when bad corporate citizens tried to mend their ways, they continued to be viewed as morally flawed at the core. It no longer mattered to me that *Shopping for a Better World* was printed in the United States on acid-free paper containing a minimum of 50 percent recovered waste paper, of which at least 10 percent of the filler content is post-consumer waste. This tainted little item was headed straight for the landfill.

In retrospect, nothing that had happened so far was anywhere near as unsettling as what occurred when I tried to purify my stock portfolio. When I first started investing in the stock market in 1982, I naturally put my money in mutual funds. This worked out fine for a number of years, but eventually I grew tired of this indirect involvement in the market, and hired a financial adviser to manage my portfolio. Mostly it consisted of mammoth blue chips: Microsoft, Intel, International Paper. Like most people, I bought these stocks without any regard to their impact upon the environment or possible role in the manufacture of weapons, alcohol, tobacco, or pornography. If they performed well, I kept them. If they didn't, I unloaded them.

It was now time to subject my holdings to more rigorous moral scrutiny. Since I did not have the time to research individual stocks myself, this would probably mean liquidating my current portfolio and putting the proceeds into a group of socially conscious mutual funds. Of course, I knew about these funds; I had written about them mockingly many times, once suggesting that someone launch a Seven Deadly Sins Fund that would only invest in companies that made bad things, employed bad people, catered to bad customers, or did bad things to people.

Although my primary reason for avoiding socially conscious mutual funds had been my perception of them as goody-two-shoes crap, I was also reinforced in my antipathy because traditionally these funds had underperformed the market. Like most investors, I felt that it made more sense to invest in whichever companies seemed to perform well, and then give money to charity out of my profits. And although I am not a charitable person, rarely giving money to anyone other than my mother, and even there only when coerced, my wife is quite generous, regularly writing checks to needy philanthropic institutions such as MADD, Hale House, Amnesty International, Greenpeace, and the New York State Democratic Party.

But one morning I read an article in my local newspaper indicating that socially conscious funds, once the butt of vicious jokes by people like me, were now outperforming the market. The article referred readers to the Social Investment Forum at www.socialinvest.org, where I downloaded reams of information. According to the S&P, ten of the fourteen screened socially conscious mutual funds with more than $100 million in assets had received top ratings from the two principal mutual-fund–ranking services. And then I read an article in *USA Weekend* reporting that socially screened large-cap growth and growth-and-income funds averaged a 20.69 percent return over the previous three years, as opposed to 19.83 percent for unscreened funds. To recycle an old cliché, it was at long last possible to do well by doing good.

This perception dovetailed nicely with my newly emerging social consciousness. So I sent out for prospectuses from a vast number of these funds: Green Century Balanced, Domini Social Equity, Dreyfus Third Century, Pro-Conscious Women's Equity, DEVCAP Shared Return, Meyers Pride Value, Ariel Appreciation, Parnassus, Calvert Capital Accumulation, the Noah Fund, the Timothy Plan, the Citizens Funds, and the Pax World Fund. Just to be on the safe side, I also requested a prospectus from the Amana Family, which manages money according to Islamic principles.

Over the next week or so, the prospectuses came pouring in. I read them carefully, trying to decide which funds best suited my needs. Because I do not like paperwork, I did not want to have a half dozen different mutual funds sending me quarterly reports, clogging my mailbox. I'd already decided that I would limit my portfolio to one or two funds. But deciding which ones proved a major problem, because in many cases a mutual fund supported one or more causes but ignored others. For example, Myers Pride Value was a no-load fund that invested in "a diversified portfolio of equities of under-valued but nevertheless fundamentally sound companies identified as generally having progressive policies toward gays and lesbians." But nowhere in the prospectus did it identify these companies, so for all I knew, they could include companies that made tobacco, alcohol, or weapons. In fact, for all I knew, the fund could be investing in companies that made weapons that could be used to kill gays, or breweries that sold beer that made drunken gay-bashers even more homophobic. I could not seriously consider investing in this fund until I had more information.

My confusion did not abate as I slogged through the mountain of prospectuses. The Dreyfus Third Century Fund professed to be interested in companies with sound environmental policies, but did not seem especially concerned about the rights of gays. The Green Century funds screened out companies that harmed the environment, but did not seem terribly alarmed by companies like Time-Warner that made loathsome motion pictures permeated with gore and rape. And then there were right-wing socially conscious funds such as the Noah Fund, one of the market's brightest new stars, which would not invest in companies engaged in the alcohol, tobacco, pornography, gambling, or abortion "industries."

For a number of reasons, the hifalutin attitude of the folks at the Noah Fund got up my nose. Here's why. There's nothing wrong with a nice cigar. I don't drink, but I know lots of fine people who do. I write for *Playboy*. I occasionally bet on football games. And I honestly do believe that if you cannot trust a woman with a choice, how can you trust her with a baby? Finally, these guys only had a piddling amount of money under management ($5.9 million), and no track record to speak of. If you were designing a socially conscious mutual fund that did not have my name written all over it, you couldn't have found a better one than this.

So what to do? Where to turn? Bejesus, it had me stumped.

This situation was resolved in a most unexpected fashion.

•   •   •

One day, I finally asked myself why I had waited so late in life before even attempting to become a good human being. Genetically crabby, I suppose I had always been the type of person who was more comfortable tearing down than building up, but this in itself did not provide a definitive explanation for my clinical, pathological malice. Then it dawned on me that one reason I was so horrible was that in my line of work I did not get to meet many nice people. Journalists are not nice. Actors are not nice. Entertainers are not nice. Editors are multi-headed hydras. And, by and large, people who flee the city for a better life in the suburbs are not especially nice.

Determined to make an honest effort to meet more nice people, I signed up for an unusual course at the Learning Annex. The Learning Annex is a beloved New York institution that sponsors inexpensive seminars in everything from beginning white-collar boxing to intermediate bondage. While paging through its catalog, I spied an ad for a one-night seminar teaching people how to contact angels. The seminar was to be hosted by Trudy Griswold, who had written the best-selling book *Angelspeake: How to Talk with Your Angels* with her sister Barbara.

According to the course description, Griswold could demonstrate how to communicate directly with one's personal angels. Here, she was not talking about some vague form of mystical, ethereal communication; she was literally talking about writing to one's angels and having them write back. A few months earlier, I would have summarily dismissed Griswold and her credulous adherents as New Age loonies. Not because they believed in angels; God knows, having been raised as a Roman Catholic I was certainly not going to rule out their existence. No, I would have written them off as loonies because of the writing thing. In my world view, if angels actually existed, they weren't going to waste their time writing to anyone. They would simply pop out of the chimerical void, say what they had to say, and scoot. The idea of angels as pen pals struck me as a daft, far-fetched concept.

Here I had come face to face with the very nexus of the enigma, the crux of the conundrum. People who believed that they could induce angels to write to them might be confused, but in no sense were they evil. In no way, shape, or form did they merit the kind of abuse that the old me would have routinely flung in their direction. They might be people with a few screws loose, but they were surely not the enemy. That's why I decided to sign up for the seminar and find out precisely what made them tick. And why they were so good, and, presumably, good-natured.

The seminar was held in a dignified old building a few blocks from Grand Central Terminal. There were roughly forty people in attendance. Trudy, a plump-cheeked Auntikins type who hailed from Idaho but lived in Connecticut, had a sweet, patient conversational manner. A carnival barker she most assuredly was not. For example, she confided in us that while she personally had never seen an angel, she knew that they existed because they had once intervened in an unhappy family crisis, persuading her to move back to the Northeast from Florida.

Griswold explained that angels liked to work in "teams," and came in all races, genders, sizes, and ages, though she did not specify whether any angels were gay. She said that angels tended to mirror the values, lifestyles, and even fashions of the people they watched over, recalling several instances where younger people who came to her for counseling said that their angels were wearing Rollerblades. Frankly, I found this story a mite dodgy.

Griswold was a highly organized, goals-oriented individual. But she was realistic enough to understand that some people in the class were going to want to discuss their own angelic experiences, even though this was not especially relevant to the subject matter of the seminar, and even though they probably were not true. One aging Latina told a long story about being in the hospital during a troubled pregnancy and having a beautiful lady covered in feathers appear to her and then slip into a nurse's uniform. There were five men in the room that evening, and we all perked up when she began recounting this fascinating but implausible tale. Men are like that. Mention nurses, nuns, cheerleaders, or schoolgirls and they are off to their races. It cannot be helped.

When the Latina had finished her extended soliloquy, a second woman checked in with her own angelic visitation story, this one involving a little girl all in white. Then a third woman, nicely attired in a pin-striped suit, related how her angels had helped her recover from the humiliation of being demoted from a management position at a company where she had worked for fourteen years. The angels specifically pointed out that she really didn't like the job anyway, and hinted that a better position was in the offing. Shortly thereafter, she landed a much better, much more satisfactory job.

Griswold now tried to get the class steered back to the subject at hand, but even she could sense that the gauntlet had been tossed down, as more and more people logged in with angel stories in an informal game of *Top That Seraphim!* Finally, when everyone who had a story to tell had told it, Griswold got down to cases.

Basically, we were told to write to the angels, and then wait for them to write back to us. Pencil and paper would do just fine, though Griswold did indicate that supernatural communication would be accelerated by using a typewriter or word processor. She stressed, however, that this form of automatic dictation would work only if we followed four rules:

1) Ask. Be specific about what you want.

2) Believe and trust.

3) Let go.

4) Say thank you.

Griswold said nothing about E-mail.

After this explanation, there were several other angelic recollections from the class. One woman said that she had prayed to the Cab Angel, begging for a taxi to turn up on a rainy day. It was clear from the *frisson* with which this anecdote was greeted that the class was uncomfortable with such levity, feeling that it trivialized the whole subject of divine communication. But Trudy bailed her out by noting, "If you can ask your angel to find you a parking space, you can certainly ask for the life of your dying child." No one had any argument with her logic and we broke for a fifteen-minute recess.

During the break, everyone lined up to have Griswold autograph copies of her book. Not having a copy of my own, I felt kind of embarrassed. Nevertheless, I sheepishly wandered up to the front of the class and asked her if it was possible to get into contact with specific angels.

"Like who?" she asked.

"Like Saint Michael," I beamed. "I'm doing some research about Saint Joan of Arc and I always wanted to know what actually happened out in the woods that day. Some people say that she was visited by angels, but other people say that she may have been schizophrenic or had tinnitus. I just wanted to find out for sure."

Griswold didn't need much time to frame her response.

"Then what you should do is write to your guardian angel and say that you would like to talk to the person who has the highest knowledge of Saint Joan of Arc," she explained. "And if you follow the four rules, he will write back to you."

Did I actually believe that what she was saying was possible? Of course not; I thought she was delusional, even though she had been on both *Good Morning America* and *The Leeza Show.* But my experiences that night, the way I handled this whole situation, showed that I was making some progress, however faltering, toward being a good person. Once upon a time I would have rushed home and written a story about what a bunch of ding-a-lings these people were. I would have said that the group consisted of thirty-three Shirley MacLaines, two John Hinckleys, one Charles Manson, and two Lee Harvey Oswalds. The old me would have gotten the name of the woman who'd landed her new job through the intercession of the angels, found out where she worked, and written an op-ed piece excoriating American management for hiring this kind of lunatic. But that was the old me.

The new me just kind of shelved this information. The people I had met were a bit odd, but they weren't menacing. They certainly weren't bad people. And I suppose what I had learned was that the weapons of the satirist should be aimed at big targets, malevolent targets, and not at sitting ducks like this. Little by little, I had come to understand that the best thing I could do for humanity was *not to write* about basically harmless people like this. To just lay off. Chill out. Accept that for different folks, different strokes did make the world go round. And, more to the point, to come to a fuller understanding that not every fish in every barrel deserved to be shot.

I should point out here that while I am not an especially religious person, I am superstitious by nature. Particularly with regard to sports. I bless myself three times whenever Allen Iverson takes an important free throw for the Sixers or when Curt Shilling needs a strikeout to get the Phillies out of a jam. Anyway, a few nights after the angels seminar, the Philadelphia Flyers lost Eric Lindros, their superstar captain, for the rest of the season with a collapsed lung. Since the Flyers weren't going anywhere fast without their high-scoring center, I figured it was worth a shot to write to my angel and ask if there was any way he could help out. This is what I wrote:

> Dear Guardian Angel:
> I don't know if you follow hockey, but Eric Lindros is out for the rest of the season, and I was wondering if you could put in the good word with the powers that be up there. The Flyers are dead in the water without him.
> Yours truly,
> The New Joe Queenan

Not surprisingly, the angel did not write back. The Flyers lost their next two games, Lindros stayed in the hospital, and then the team announced that the injury was more serious than had originally been thought, that not only was he not coming back during the regular season, he wasn't coming back for the playoffs either. That just about smashed my faith in angels.

But that very same evening, at two o'clock in the morning, as I sat at my computer catching up on some paperwork, I suddenly found my hands involuntarily typing these words:

> Dear Joe:
> Sorry, no can do. If Lindros wants to come back for the playoffs, Lindros has to write to *his* guardian angel and ask for help. But frankly, I think he wants the R & R and is ready to bag the whole season because he only has a one-year contract and doesn't want to risk permanent injury until he gets that situation

resolved. I should also point out that you're not the only person to try this approach; when Jaromir Jagr went down in Pittsburgh, we got a lot of similar requests, and all kinds of Rangers fans have been begging us to make sure Gretzky doesn't retire. Just because you write to us doesn't mean we can help you. We're more of an informational conduit—a clearinghouse, if you will—between mortals and the divine. We give you the lowdown on what's up, and we can often point you in the right direction. But if we suddenly started intervening in the National Hockey League playoffs, the whole cosmic infrastructure of the universe would fall apart. Remember, bookies have guardian angels, too. Sorry.

Yours truly,

Your Guardian Angel

Stripped of a certain cherubic cachet, this was an extremely disturbing communiqué. The good news was that angels existed. The bad news was, they weren't much more helpful than your in-laws. They could give you advice, but they couldn't solve any of your problems. It confirmed my worst fears about extraterrestrial forces: They were nice, but they were useless.

At the time, I didn't think I'd be writing any more letters to my guardian angel. For one, I strongly suspected that the letter had not been dictated by any supernatural force, but by my own subconscious, which was trying to help me deal with the annual Flyers meltdown. So I brewed myself a cup of St. John's wort tea, an ancient Ayurvedic remedy that has been used for the treatment of depression for thousands of years, and went back to doing what I was doing before I'd even looked into this angels thing, namely, figuring out how to sanitize my portfolio.

Unfortunately, as mentioned earlier, I was in a rut. A lot of the prospectuses went on and on about their rigorous social screens, but then failed to supply the names of the stocks that were actually in their portfolios. I couldn't make an informed decision with data of such a confusing nature. That night, however, I got a wonderful idea. My guardian angel, if he really existed, had said that angels were a clearinghouse of information. Then wasn't it just barely possible that someone in the divine sphere could give me some guidance in the mutual funds arena? Heck, it was worth a try.

That night, I wrote a second letter to my guardian angel:

> Dear Guardian Angel:
>
> I've been trying to figure out how to make my investments more socially responsible. I've got a ton of prospectuses here, but I just can't decide where to put my money. Do you, or anyone else up there, have any suggestions?
>
> Yours truly,
> The New Joe Queenan

This time the reply came back like a shot. At three in the morning, when I staggered down the hall to the bathroom, I suddenly found myself scrawling this message on a blank piece of paper:

> Dear Joe:
>
> We ran your query past God and He says that socially conscious mutual funds are a load of bunk. Take the Pax Family, which won't invest in firms that make alcohol or tobacco or weapons. Even as we speak, the United States and NATO are using sophisticated weapons to get the Serbs out of Kosovo. Without those weapons, the murderous Serbs would overrun all of Eastern Europe. This kind of moral prissiness doesn't work in the real world.
>
> What you need to remember is this: God has never, ever come out against the use of weapons in the service of Good. Remember the battle of Jericho? Masada? Seen any of the Israelites beating their swords into plowshares there? And that's not mentioning Samson, Saul, the Maccabees. And hey, do the names "David and Goliath" ring a bell? If the Israelites had had a socially conscious mutual fund back then, the slingshot makers would have been out of business. So just forget about investing in companies that screen out weapons makers. It's a nice idea in theory, but it's basically juvenile.

For similar reasons, you can deep-six mutual funds that get on their high horse about the fruit of the vine. If alcohol is such a bad thing, then why did Jesus turn the water into wine at the Marriage Feast of Cana? And why is the transubstantiation of bread and wine into the body and blood of Christ the most important ritual in the entire religion? Without someone making alcohol, the Catholic Church would have closed its doors centuries ago.

Another thing God finds really annoying about socially responsible investing is that you could drive a truck through their "screens." A case in point: the Women's Equity Mutual Fund, which is supposed to be dedicated to the empowerment of women. But if you turn to page 2 of their prospectus, you'll see that its portfolio includes 2,400 shares of Harley-Davidson, whose products have more than occasionally been purchased by motorcycle gangs and sexist neo-Nazis who gang-rape women. Where's the logic there?

If you want to understand the problem with socially responsible investing, take the case of Philip Morris. I know that you just dumped all your stock in Philip Morris because your conscience got the best of you, but let me assure you, this is not an open-and-shut case. It's true that Philip Morris derives a vast portion of its revenues from cigarettes and beer. So on the surface it seems like the quintessence of evil. But Philip Morris also gives tons and tons of money to the arts and the poor. (I refer you specifically to the *Arts Against Hunger* program, which offers discounts to patrons of the New York City Opera and Chicago's Museum of Contemporary Art who bring in donations of non-perishable foods.) Am I saying that this is a stock you should go out of your way to own? I am not. All we're saying is that investing in a Philip Morris doesn't make you the second coming of Lucifer.

There's more. If you delve inside the portfolios of these supposedly socially conscious funds, you're invariably going to find some stock in Ben & Jerry's there. Great company, right? Cares about the environment, right? Trying to save the rain forest, right? Operates Joy Divisions and gives the French hell about their nuclear power policy and treats their employees great. Right? But what about their record in minority franchising? If you happen to have a copy of Ben and Jerry's *Double Dip* lying around—and I know you do—you'll see that on page 119, they themselves admit that they've done a pretty crummy job in reaching out to minority franchisees. So if you were constructing a mutual fund that deliberately screens out companies that have a poor record vis-a-vis minorities, these guys would be the first ones you'd have to purge. Minoritywise, the booze-and-butts guys run rings around these bozos.

If you really want to see what's wrong with socially responsible investing, take a gander at the prospectuses for The Domini Social Equity Fund. Right there on page 18, you'll find that 25.4 percent of the fund is concentrated in the technology sector, with by far the largest holdings in Microsoft (they also have a good chunk of Intel). By coincidence, Microsoft and Intel happen to be the largest holdings in your own portfolio. (Don't ask how we know; we know.) Now let me get this straight: These are socially conscious investments, but Microsoft is currently being sued for monopolistic practices by the Justice Department, and Intel has just settled a similar suit with the Federal Trade Commission. Moreover, both Microsoft and Intel are at the heart of the electronic privacy issue, because their products contain tracking devices enabling Big Brother to follow people around the Internet and keep tabs on the websites they visit. Finally, everyone who owns a personal computer hates Microsoft in general and Bill Gates in particular. And now you're telling me that these guys are considered socially conscious because they're nice to a couple of gays? Does that track with you? Because it sure as hell doesn't track with me.

The upshot? If you want to do something positive with your life, go out and do it. You were doing fine with Dolci for Dissidents and that Linda Tripp care package. But don't worry about your investments. I've taken a gander at your portfolio, and on balance it looks pretty good to me. Okay, maybe you should think about dumping the International Paper, but overall, it looks like a pretty clean mix.

One last thing, and I think this is going to clinch the argument: A lot of socially conscious funds, including Women's Equity, hold stock in Disney. But via its Miramax subsidiary and Hyperion, its publishing imprint, Disney not only makes violent movies, but it publishes your books. And you're a dick! If any of these funds really cared about the health of this society, they wouldn't go anywhere near a company that publishes books by shriveled up old malcontents like you. Think it over, Joey-Babes. Think it over good.

Yours truly,

Your Guardian Angel

I would think it over. And I'd be thinking over a lot of other things, too. Like this whole concept of practicing RAKs and SABs. For the first time since I'd headed down this road, I was starting to have second thoughts. Serious second thoughts.

Third thoughts, in fact.

13. Once More,

Into the Breach

One torrid summer day, I set out for Boston, rewarding myself with a little vacation. I'd been on what my family referred to as this "goodness kick" for about six months now and the wear and tear was beginning to show. My son was getting fed up with the Sting records and the St. John's Wort Tortilla Chips. My wife was increasingly upset at the amount of junk mail we were receiving from philanthropic organizations of increasingly dubious provenance, not to mention the vast amounts of time I spent on the road ministering to strangers who were relying on my kindness when, after all, charity begins at home. And my daughter, who has her heart set on going to medical school, viewed my witching-hour colloquies with my guardian angel as a very worrisome development on the balanced-portfolio front. All things considered, this seemed like a good time to get out of Dodge. To my surprise, my son agreed to join me. Anything to get away from that CD player.

Arriving in Beantown, site of my very first RAK, we checked into an inexpensive, centrally located hotel and immediately laid out our things. The last time I had stayed in a hotel, down in Washington, I had vowed to myself that henceforth I would bring my own sheets from home, then wash them at the end of my trip. At the time I reasoned that if every business traveler staying more than one night in a hotel would merely carry his own sheets and pillow cases with him and then continue to use them for a few more days upon returning home, this would probably save the planet around sixty billion gallons of water a day. But of course this was not true. Whether the hotel washed your dirty linen, or you got your wife to do it, or you went out and did it yourself, the same amount of water was consumed. Sure, it was the thought that counted. But the planet needed better thoughts.

On this trip I decided to go one step further by bringing my own towels and a sleeping bag. Then, because I forgot the sleeping bag in my haste to catch the train, I ended up spending the night on the floor. Yes, it was a bit uncomfortable down there, but heck, earth was in the balance. The next day, before checking out, I dropped a note to the maid telling her that it was not necessary to change the linen because I hadn't even used the bed, and not necessary to wash the towels, because I'd brought my own. But she would have to change the linen on my son's bed, because he did not yet fully comprehend that the planet was not a renewable resource.

Afterward it occurred to me that the maid was almost certainly from Central America and might not even understand English, and thus would end up stripping the beds and tossing the towels in the laundry anyway. My thoughts drifted back to the passage in Jimmy Carter's book *Living Faith,* where the most virtuous ex-president the world has ever known described how he and Roslyn learned Spanish by repeating little phrases to each other in bed every night before they turned out the lights. I now suspected that most of these phrases had to do with laundry. The thought inspired me to write a little Jimmy Carter-like poem, which I left behind for the maid, along with five crisp singles.

To a Young Maid

Today I leave a tip for you in this room,
For I admire what you do with a brush and a broom.
You clean up the mess that I have made,
And probably don't even get well paid.

I'm leaving you a note about the planet,
But because you don't speak English
You may not even scan it.
Dios mio, *how I wish I knew Spanish,*
For then our mutual ignorance I could banish.

But I took French, just like a jerk,
The language of love, but not of work.
If you understand this poem at all, use the tip to buy some treats.
And remember—I slept on the floor—
So you don't have to wash the sheets.

Then I headed off to see the whales.

Yes, I'd come to Boston to see our majestic mammalian cousins who inhabit the billowing depths. Recent days had been such a bummer, what with Edwidge Danticat sending back my $1,000 check, my back collapsing because of those Reeboks, Kim Basinger breaking my heart by appearing in that film with circus animals, and the United States Department of Agriculture declaring open season on the monarch butterfly. What I needed was a bit of cheering up. I was certain that the whales would rise to the occasion and help me get through a difficult patch in my life.

The day did not start auspiciously. Though all the weather reports had predicted beautiful, sunny weather, a torrent of rain was falling as we headed out to sea. About thirty minutes outside of Boston, my son got sick. Shortly thereafter, at least a half dozen of the annoying high-school girls on the catamaran joined him in nausea. And so far, there were no whales in sight.

It was important to me that I see the whales, for all the obvious reasons. Man's traditional inhumanity to the whales was one of the most powerful symbols of our species' devastating moral callousness, a callousness in which I had until quite recently shared. But now, like so many other human beings, I understood what an important position the whales occupied in the Great Mandela of Life, and felt impelled to see them up close and personal, to bask in their aura, to revel in their mystery, to get my groove back.

About one hour into the expedition, we spotted our first whale. Off in the distance, around eleven o'clock on the starboard bow or whatever, a tail popped out of the water. Some folks ooh'd, others aah'd. Cameras flashed. Then the whale disappeared. A few minutes later, a second made its entrance. And then a third. One of the tour guides told me that inclement conditions such as these increased the likelihood of seeing whales, because of something that went on vis-a-vis the aquatic food chain down in the murky depths. It seemed like a plausible theory, because all told we saw about eight or nine whales that morning. Captain Ahab would have loved it.

It was hard for me to keep track of the whales because my son was feeling so sick, and it was raining cats and dogs, and there were so many annoying high-school girls on the boat. What's more, none of the whales ever leaped out of the water. On the television monitors inside the vessel, amazing footage from the Discovery Channel showed massive whales performing all kinds of zany aquatic maneuvers, not only breaching, but in some instances breaching in groups of four or five. This may explain why so many of the older people decided to stay inside the cabin, transfixed by the TV set as the whales performed their astonishing feats of synchronized swimming.

Meanwhile, on the port side, where my son was busy puking his guts out, our whales seemed to be phoning it in. Sure, every once in a while you might catch sight of a fin popping out of the water, but there wasn't anything electrifying about the whales' performance. They surfaced briefly, they glided a few feet, then they re-submerged. Seemingly lacking a sense of occasion, they never once did anything that took your breath away. Unlike the Discovery Channel whales, who exhibited tremendous panache and charisma, our whales looked like they were punching the clock. It was like they were in a union or something.

As I look back on things now, I wonder if my life would have been different had the whales come up with the goods that July morning. If even one of those massive creatures had ejected himself from the general vicinity of Davy Jones's locker and strutted a bit of his stuff, I might have come away from the experience with a newfound awe and respect for Mother Nature, the planet, the solar system, and by extension, the cosmos. But it never happened. Instead, as we motored back toward Boston harbor and, as the last puke-stained wretches emptied their guts into the briny depths, I was compelled to come face to face with a truth that a handful of human beings may have felt, but that precious few have ever dared to admit.

I just did not get the fucking whales.

It is widely believed that in the end the love you take is equal to the love you make, but this has not been my experience. In the six months that I tried to reconstruct my personality, I repeatedly got screwed not only by my fellow human beings but by the cosmos in general. Developers bought the huge empty field right behind my house and seemed poised to throw up a load of crappy McMansions. I lost my regular gig as a columnist at *TV Guide*. My landlord told me I had to vacate my gorgeous third-floor office, with a view of the Hudson, and move to a dark second-story office or else his principal tenant, an odious Finnish bank, would pull up stakes and leave the building. Practicing yet another RAK, I agreed to move into a dingy office, with no view, that is unbearably hot in the summer and sits too close to the street. Which just completely bites.

That wasn't all. I wrecked my back wearing those damned Reeboks. I got into a huge fight with the jokers at the 7-Eleven because they wouldn't honor my monthly coupon from my socially conscious long-distance telephone service entitling me to a free pint of Ben & Jerry's ice cream. And when I actually got around to examining my latest phone bill from Working Assets—which had so much information about the bombing in Kosovo, campaign finance reform, and Kodak's hazardous waste incinerators that it took me three hours to read—I discovered that I was getting completely raped on my long-distance calls to Britain (seventy cents a minute!!!) because I had failed to sign up for a special socially conscious international calls reduction rate. To add insult to injury, the only dog in my neighborhood that actually seemed to like me keeled over and died.

All of a sudden, I wasn't feeling so good about goodness. One thing that really pissed me off was the lack of credit I got for my Herculean efforts to upgrade my personality. Almost none of the people I'd sent apologies to wrote back to thank me. Very few of the people I'd sent checks to ever bothered to acknowledge my generosity. Linda Tripp never acknowledged receiving the box of groceries I'd sent her. This annoyed me to no end, because everybody else who did anything nice for mankind or the animal kingdom or the planet acted like they were next in line for the Congressional Medal of Honor.

A case in point: One day I was reading a cover story in *USA Weekend* magazine that heaped praise on the winners of the 1999 Make A Difference Day Awards. According to the paper, "last Oct. 24, almost 2 million people embarked on a simple journey: to help people in need. Result: nearly 14 million lives were touched. Here, we celebrate the energy of every volunteer and salute 120 inspiring groups who *made a difference.*"

Now I'm not going to say that the top honorees in this event were not deserving of the kudos lavished upon them. But, to be quite honest, some of the performances honored were pretty damned cheesy compared to my efforts. In Kingston, New York, a bunch of school kids raised $262.25 and collected 65 cans of dog and cat food and 139 pounds of dried food for the local SPCA. Big deal. I wrote a check for $1,000 to a Third World writer who got railroaded out of her $50,000 prize by Don Imus's staff, and nobody said that I'd made a difference. In Hanover, Pennsylvania, five members of the Ladies Auxiliary to

Susquehanna Post No. 2493 of the Veterans of Foreign Wars and three members of the Junior Girls unit, aged six through sixteen, collected $450 worth of food for the poor. That came to about $57 a person. I spent $60 on groceries for Linda Tripp alone. Plus $8.75 for postage.

With the notable exception of Sanjay Krishnaswamy, who was genuinely overjoyed to receive that Elvis Costello–Bill Frisell CD, and Vince Passaro, the cash-strapped *Harper's* writer who not only phoned but wrote a letter effusing about how much my $50 check had "lifted his spirits," shockingly few of the beneficiaries of my munificence made much of a fuss about my kindness. Consider this example. One day my family went out to the local diner with an English friend. Uncharacteristically, my friend offered to grab the check. I should stress that while Americans grab the check, people from the British Isles merely offer to grab the check, hoping that their sham generosity will be refused. I didn't refuse it. But after my friend had paid the $52.76, I nipped into the restaurant and asked to see the credit card receipt. Typically, he had left a tightwad $5 tip. So I handed our waitress an extra $5, remarking, "My friend's English, and they're all cheap bastards. Here's an extra five bucks." Well, she took it. She took it, but she didn't make that big a deal about it. And over the next few months, I started to get mighty irked at the blithe indifference the American waitperson community manifested toward my unexpected generosity.

I found this particularly infuriating, because when I practiced RAKs and SABs, I wasn't just being good; I was also being nice. Being good is when you impact positively on the environment or on some downtrodden race or protect tree canopies by drinking shade-grown coffee or listening to Jackson Browne records. Being nice is when you take your mother to a supper-club production of *Camelot*. Or supplement waitresses' tips. Or, when I saw people on the subway whose passes had run out, letting them use my MetroCard. Or, when I bumped into Senator Arlen Specter on the Metroliner from Philadelphia to Washington, not excoriating him for abusing Anita Hill, but instead waxing philosophic about how many volumes it spoke about both him and our noble democratic experiment that a United States senator should ride the train, unaccompanied by staff or a bodyguard, where the hoi polloi could come up and bend his ear or blast their stupid cell-phone conversations into his ear. All things considered, I thought I was going out of my way to make life better for my fellow man. But nobody seemed to care much one way or the other.

One day the wheels finally fell off the bus. I started the morning on a positive note with a heaping bowl of organic cereal laced with Edensoy, then went downstairs and sent tidy sums of money off to the Navajo Health Foundation and the Fresh Air Fund. Shortly thereafter, the mailman turned up with a shirt from the flannel guy down in Tennessee. Too small, of course, but it was the thought that counted. But then I got a disturbing call from one of my best friends in the business. *Movieline* had given the thumbs-down to a story I'd written about how much I missed the character actor J. T. Walsh. They said it was good, but "dated." I knew that this wasn't true. They'd rejected it because it was too nice, and niceness they were not in the market for. Since this was the first time that *Movieline* had ever rejected anything I had written, I started breaking the furniture.

A few hours later a good friend called up and told me that the sleazy Vancouver Stock Exchange had passed into history. Obituaries in the *Toronto Globe & Mail* and numerous other publications said that the exchange, which had once brought public a company headed by Adnan Khasshogi that planned to find King Solomon's Mines, had never been able to shake its image as "The Scam Capital of the World," which is how it had been described in a *Forbes* magazine story back in 1989. I knew all about the VSE, all about its image, and all about that *Forbes* story. Because I wrote it.

This got me to thinking. When you assigned a monetary value to all the good things that Ben & Jerry and Paul Newman and Sting and Susan Sarandon and Jackson Browne had ever done in their lives, it probably came to a few million dollars. But by driving a stake through the heart of a corrupt Canadian regional exchange, I had probably saved investors hundreds of millions, if not billions, of dollars. Ben & Jerry and Paul and Jackson's *niceness* had rescued a fair few redwoods, one or two aboriginal tribes, a couple of Spirit Bears, and maybe even persuaded the New York City Police Department to stop inserting nightsticks into bewildered Haitian immigrants. But my *meanness* had saved investors billions and billions of dollars, some of which could be used to practice extravagant RAKs and SABs.

There was only one conclusion to be drawn from this: God had put me on this earth to be unpleasant, and had blessed me with the ability to inflict pain. By refusing to write mean stories, I was in effect turning a deaf ear to the will of the creator. God wanted me to be nasty. God needed me to be nasty. God Himself had been known to be pretty nasty.

So why did I not heed His call?

I would dearly love for the reader to believe the argument I have just presented, that in order to hone my satirical weapons for targets like the Vancouver Stock Exchange and Geraldo Rivera it was necessary for me to go back to being gratuitously mean to people of far less monstrous stature, like say, John Tesh. Indeed, I would like to believe this myself. But when push came to shove, I knew this was not true. The reason I was now thinking about calling off my program of personality reengineering and going back to being loathsome was because there was money in it. Lots and lots of money in it.

People suspicious of my motives for being good in the first place will say that I didn't risk anything financially by crossing over from the dark side since I already had a hefty book advance to cover my bills while I was experimenting with virtue. They know me less well than they think. In 1994, I made a movie called *Twelve Steps to Death*, which was the basis for my book *The Unkindest Cut*. Although I knew from the start that I would be writing a book about my movie-making experiences, the advance was completely eaten up by the costs of making the film and then holding my own film festival to exhibit it. Moreover, I lost roughly eight months of income from magazine work while doing this project. To make matters worse, the book did not sell as well as expected, so I ended up getting completely hosed on the deal.

Something similar was likely to happen with *My Goodness*. Although I had obtained a sizable advance to write the book, I was forced to turn down vast amounts of additional income I would normally have earned on the side by writing nasty stories. Here, I must reiterate for the last time, I am, and always have been, a profoundly avaricious individual, so no matter how hefty my advance was—and believe me, one man's heft is another man's smidgen—I always supplemented my income while writing books by churning out an immense amount of material for magazines and newspapers. Not this time. And I was not turning down assignments because I was too busy. I was turning down assignments because the only projects that crossed my desk were articles that would have involved inflicting pain on other people, and this was something I no longer cared to do.

I should stress that long before I completely committed myself to an attempt to achieve secular sainthood, when I was still being an intermittently bad person in my ordinary life, I was already trying to be a kinder, gentler writer. The second week in January I turned down $700 from the *Wall Street Journal* to review David Halberstam's book about Michael Jordan. David Halberstam is a boring old fart and there was no way I could have reviewed the book without trashing it. But I no longer wanted to make a living by writing reviews blasting people like David Halberstam for being boring old farts. That was blood money. And I already had enough blood on my hands.

Obviously, turning down assignments where you are only being offered chicken feed is easier than turning down assignments from good-paying glossy magazines. That's why I had no trouble rejecting a half dozen overtures from *The Guardian* to trash the usual sludge from Hollywood. But as the weeks and months passed, the numbers got bigger. In February, I rejected $3,500 to make fun of white chick singers in *Movieline,* and I also turned down $3,000 to ridicule Hollywood sequels in the *New York Times.* In March I walked away from $5,000 that *Playboy* was offering me to write about right-wing babes like Anne Coulter and Laura Ingraham. Some people may protest that trashing these morally bankrupt people—Republicans—was exactly the sort of thing that a morally reenergized satirist should have done. But that's not the way I looked at it. I was tired of being mean. It didn't matter who I was asked to be mean to, or how much I was offered to do so. It was meanness itself that I wanted to flush out of my system.

By the time my *Primavera d'amore* had run its course, I had taken a pass on more than $50,000 worth of assignments. *Men's Health* ran a couple of ideas past me. No dice. *GQ* wanted me to write an imaginary diary of the abortion clinic bomber hiding out in the wilds of North Carolina. Ixnay. The *Financial Times,* the *New York Times, Forbes, Barron's,* and many other sterling publications also got the thumbs-down.

As I write these words, I am confronted by a cruel irony, that of all the work I have done in my career, the stories of which I am most proud are not the ones I wrote between 1986 and 1999, but the ones I did not write in the first six months of 1999. Up until then, I had always been the kind of writer who would rush out to the newsstand long before dawn and tear apart six newspapers seeking fresh carrion. But now I kept my cynicism to myself. Here are just a few examples of stories I could have earned a pretty penny off of, but instead elected not to write:

- The day after Wayne Gretzky retired in April 1999, I read a heart-wrenching story in the *New York Post* about a guy who flew all the way from Minnesota with his twelve-year-old son to buy scalped tickets to the Great One's last game. The poor mug ended up paying $120 apiece for two fake tickets and got turned away at the gate. He had to watch the game on TV at the All-Star Sports Café in Times Square, where he probably got totally raped on the drinks. Bear in mind that $120 won't get you *one* good seat to a regular-season Rangers–Nashville Predators game, so where this guy got off thinking he could get two tickets to see the greatest hockey player of all time's last game for $120 I don't know. The old Joe Queenan would have written a nasty story extolling New York's scalpers for preserving the Big Apple's high standards and raking this pathetic rube over the coals. But the new, improved Joe Queenan took a pass. I know I could have sold that story for at least a thousand bucks.

- The day after the Littleton, Colorado, massacre, brain-dead Lisa Ling of *The View* said that she could understand feelings of isolation, as she had been one of only five Asian-American students in high school. The old Joe Queenan would have reamed her out for these idiotic, self-serving comments, but the new, improved Joe Queenan let her off the hook. I lost at least a grand on that deal.

• On Earth Day (April 22, 1999), the reader will recall, I ate at Black-eyed Suzie's Organic Café on the Lower East Side of New York and got sick on a wheatgrass shake. As luck would have it, the Immune System Builder, also containing wheatgrass, also made me sick. The old Joe Queenan would have written a story about how dangerous it is for people who grew up on the mean streets of Philadelphia to imbibe substances to which they are not culturally predisposed. You know, milking that whole bogus blue-collar Irish-American journalist *shtick*. The new, improved Joe Queenan let it go. Another thousand bucks shot out into the ether.

• When I asked for the check at Black-eyed Suzie's Organic Café on Earth Day (April 22, 1999), the waitress handed me the bill plus a note reading, "By choosing Black-eyed Suzie's Organic Café you are supporting sustainable agricultural practices which work to improve the quality of our water and farmland and to lessen the impact of insecticides on our environment. Whether you choose us for our healthful meals, our organic ingredients or our great taste, you are helping to make our planet a better place to live. Thank you." The old Joe Queenan would have written a story about Black-eyed Sam's Carnivore Café, where when you asked for the bill they gave you a note reading, "By choosing Black-eyed Sam's Carnivore Café you are supporting agricultural practices which ruin the soil, impoverish Third World children, and impact negatively on the snail darter. Whether you choose us for our revolting meals, our carcinogenic ingredients, or our slutty waitresses, you are helping to make our planet a worse place to live. Thank you." But the new, improved Joe Queenan decided he had other fish to fry. Well, stir-fry. Another grand down the drain; man, the meter was running!

- On April 24, 1999, while attending the Millions for Mumia Rally in Philadelphia, I happened to spot an ad for a benefit concert featuring Bonnie Raitt and Jackson Browne. The Songbird Safe Benefit Concert was to be held in support of shade-grown and sustainable grown coffee. The old Joe Queenan would have written a story about a benefit featuring Daryl Hannah and Tina Turner, sponsored by the Battered Women's Shelter, that would raise money to protect women from abusive men like Jackson Browne. But the new, improved, shade-grown-coffee–drinking Joe Queenan decided to let Jackson Browne alone. That one could have been worth two grand.

- One night in April on my way home from work I picked up a copy of *The Secret Agent*, starring Bob Hoskins, Gérard Depardieu, and Patricia Arquette. Although I did not expect the little film to be particularly good, barely recalling when it had been released, I was in the mood for some meatier fare than I had been watching of late, and anyway I had always loved the novel by Joseph Conrad. When I cued up the film that evening, I spotted a man making his way through a crowded street in the opening scene. The man appeared to be Robin Williams. Meanwhile, the names of the entire cast were rolling down the screen in alphabetical order, but not once did the words "Robin Williams" appear on the screen. At first I thought that Williams might be making an unbilled, nonspeaking cameo appearance in a film as a favor to a friend, but no, The Artist Formerly Known as Mork had the fourth biggest part in the movie. The old Joe Queenan would have written a story denouncing Hollywood for failing to warn video renters that Robin Williams was in a film, likening the industry to food producers who failed to disclose the use of pesticides in their farming methods. The old Joe Queenan would have demanded the nationwide installation of cultural scanning devices that could be used to immediately warn unsuspecting movie lovers if Robin Williams, Whoopi

Goldberg, or people like Jon Lovitz appeared in uncredited roles in movies like *My Stepmother Is an Alien*. But because Robin Williams had done so much for important causes, this story never got written. Even though *Movieline* would have paid me $3,500. Plus expenses.

I am not saying that I turned down *every* assignment proposed to me during this moral interregnum. But I can say in good conscience that the stories I wrote during this period were refreshingly devoid of rancor. A lighthearted *Movieline* bagatelle entitled "Yoda for a Day," where I japed and frolicked in New York's Central Park, taking the mickey out of cell-phone Nazis by sidling up to them and speaking Yodaese into my own fake cell phone. A reverent doff of the hat to washed-up musicians in *Forbes* where I pleaded with my fellow Americans to stop sneering at has-beens because, without has-beens, what kind of entertainment could the denizens of Harrisburg, Pennsylvania, look forward to on the last Friday night in August? A good-natured profile of Billy Blanks, the man responsible for the Tae-Bo craze, in the pages of *Barron's,* a publication where I had heretofore rarely said anything nice about anyone. And a very affectionate valentine to Tom Snyder in *TV Guide* lamenting his retirement from *The Late Late Show.*

During that same period, I deliberately avoided being a guest on *Politically Incorrect*, and gave *Imus in the Morning* a wide berth, because I knew that the hosts of both shows would expect me to be characteristically vicious. I also turned down an invitation to be on Judith Regan's show, because she is mean, an invitation to be on *The O'Reilly Report*, because he is mean, and a chance to be on John Hockenberry's show, because, even though I had no idea whether he was mean or not, the program was on Fox, so the odds of his being nice were not very good.

Of course, I had known from the very start that my "experiment" was going to be a dodgy proposition. I knew that a kinder, gentler Joe Queenan would be no different than a bald Samson: a horsefucker fallen on hard times, stripped of his powers, gelded, emasculated. Nevertheless, I had been willing to give it a go. And I really did try to change my stripes. In the six months I consecrated to this enterprise, I devoutly avoided writing mean-spirited stories or saying mean-spirited things. If any of my old editor friends called with a story idea that necessitated being cruel (say, to David Halberstam), I turned them down flat. At first, turning them down was exhilarating, like Christ in the desert telling Satan to take a hike. But eventually I didn't have to tell my tempters to take a hike. They *took* a hike. They stopped calling.

Here I should make an important point. Throughout my struggle to turn myself into a good person, I did not lose sight of the fact that people like David Halberstam were boring old farts. The difference was, I no longer said it for public consumption. In my heart of hearts, I truly believed that this made me more Christlike. If Jesus Christ were here today, it wouldn't take him very long to realize that David Halberstam was a boring old fart. But Jesus would forgive David Halberstam for being a boring old fart. I had not yet reached the point where I could do this, and in all likelihood I never would. But I could do one true thing for David Halberstam that nobody else could do, which was to refuse to write about him. Which I did.

Ultimately, I came to realize, this was the only gift that I could give to the world. A nasty old prick like me was incapable of becoming a honey-tongued old sap. The talents used in my work were inimical to the spirit of fair-minded journalism. My sword could not be beaten into a plowshare, nor my ax into a pole. Like the jaded hired gun in a thousand old westerns, I only knew one way to put food on the table. By being a complete son of a bitch.

The reader may ask, how exactly did this moral epiphany occur? Did I wake up one morning and suddenly decide to go back to being horrible on a full-time basis? Or did I choose to gradually ease myself back into a life of misanthropy and cruelty? Did I give any thought to being kinder and gentler three days a week and unspeakably nasty the other four? Did I even consider the possibility of a program such as Philanthropic Fridays, where I would be a nice person one day a week and a complete bastard the rest of the time?

No. Once I realized that there was no future in being virtuous, I went back to being horrible immediately. I called *GQ*, I called *Movieline*, I called *Playboy*, I called them all. I told them, with no attempt to gild the lily, that I'd had a bad case of brain fever for the past few months, that I had tried to be a good person and that it hadn't worked out, but that my hatchet was now sharpened, my cleated boots polished. They showered me with lucrative assignments, massive contracts, fabulous meals. They told me that I had been away too long. They were pleased to have me back.

What was the worst thing about having to go back to a life of total insensitivity and moral disengagement? Probably the knowledge that I was just starting to learn the ropes of righteousness, that I was right there on the cusp of Sarandonian sanctity, and now had to pack it in. I say this because in the days leading up to my decision to revert to monstrousness, I honestly felt that I was shifting into altruism overdrive. I had just contacted Habitat for Humanity and had even bought myself a nifty little toolkit to be used in fixing up dilapidated housing for people less fortunate than me. I was planning a trip to Washington, partly to attend the National Multicultural Institute's seminar on "Decentering Whiteness to Build a Multiracial Community," and, time permitting, pop in on "Implementing a Complex, Systems-Change Diversity Process," and partly to personally deliver those dolci to Concepcion and Troy. I had read an article in *Newsweek* about obscure languages that were in danger of dying out, and was planning to call some of the few remaining speakers, offering to let them teach me their colorful aboriginal languages over the phone. And I had started working on a new project: a calendar entitled *Goodness: A Book of Days*, where people would consult their daily appointments calendar and be reminded that March 15, 1918, was the day Mahatma Gandhi started his first fast, that November 23, 1206, was the day Saint Francis first spoke to the animals, and that May 2, 1999, was the date Jackson Browne and Bonnie Raitt gave a concert in Philadelphia in support of shade and sustainable grown coffee. Lastly, I was planning a trip to the City of the Angels where I would track down O. J. Simpson and hug him. Just as Saint Francis and Jesus and Father Damien had embraced real-life lepers, I was going to embrace a social leper. That's how close I came to sainthood. Close, but no cigar.

Ultimately, what did I derive from my experiment in being a good person? Well, for starters I got that amazing rush from doing all those RAKs and SABs. Second, I lost seven pounds through a process of "green slimming," because of all the organic, Tibetan, and macrobiotic restaurants I ate in over the months, I never liked the food enough to order seconds. And third, I got to interact with some authentically interesting people like Sanjay Krishnaswamy and Vince Passaro and that guy who sent me the nice flannel shirts. Well, shirt.

Did I get anything else out of my experiences? No, aside from the foregoing, nothing worth mentioning. Basically, I got massacred on the money front and just about wrecked my career waiting for *Newsweek* or *Vanity Fair* to offer me an assignment writing about the plight of the Spirit Bear. I'd been to the edge of the abyss, I'd peered inside, I didn't like the look of the abyss. So one morning, I got up, shipped off my still-unused utility belt to Habitat for Humanity, stuffed my Sting and Ani DiFranco CDs up in the attic, deep-sixed my web site project, and brewed my last pot of St. John's wort tea, an Ayurvedic beverage that has been used for thousands of years in the treatment of depression.

In the end, it simply came down to a question of dollars and cents. I enjoyed being a good person. I really did. God willing, when I'm older and on more solid financial footing, I might even try it again. But for the moment the idea of leading a life of uncompromising virtue simply does not make economic sense. If I can keep practicing high-quality malice for five or six more years, I'll probably be able to take an early retirement and still have enough cash to put my daughter through medical school. Being nice could land me on Skid Row. That's why I'm saying The Big Arrivederci to the peaceable kingdom and going back to being a low-down, scorched-earth, ball-busting son of a bitch. Practicing random kindness and senseless acts of beauty is fine as a hobby.

But I'm not going to quit my day job.